JOHN F. KENNEDY
Scrimshaw Collector

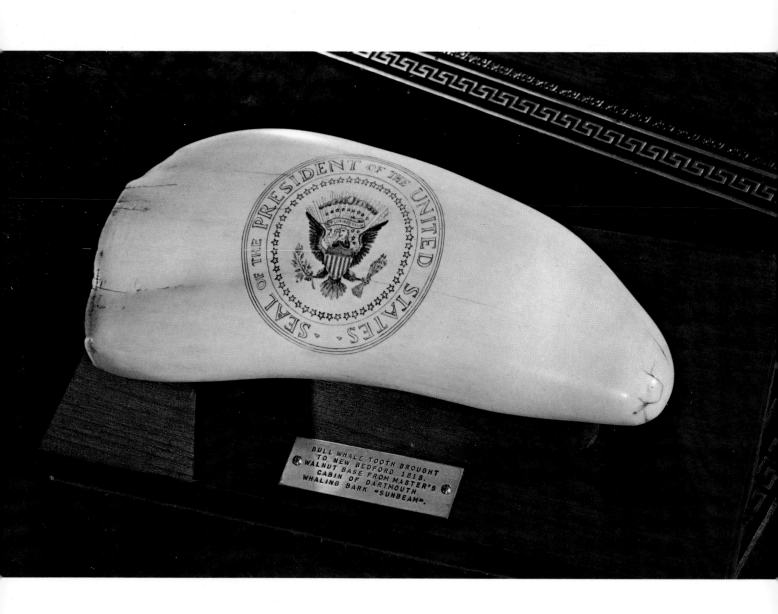

BULL WHALE TOOTH BROUGHT
TO NEW BEDFORD 1818.
WALNUT BASE FROM MASTER'S
CABIN OF DARTMOUTH
WHALING BARK "SUNBEAM".

JOHN F. KENNEDY
Scrimshaw Collector

by Clare Barnes, Jr.

PHOTOGRAPHS BY ALAN FONTAINE

LITTLE, BROWN AND COMPANY · BOSTON · TORONTO

A portion of the text of this book, together with the photographs on pages ii, vi, viii, 3, 15, 17, 18, 93, 105, and 111, appeared originally in *American Heritage*.

Published simultaneously in Canada by Little, Brown & Company (Canada) Limited

PRINTED IN THE UNITED STATES OF AMERICA

To my wife

Ships that pass in the night and speak each other in passing;

Only a signal shown and a distant voice in the darkness;

So on the ocean of life we pass and speak one another,

Only a look and a voice; then darkness again and a silence.

— HENRY WADSWORTH LONGFELLOW

Contents

The Scrimshaw Collector 1

Why did five great whales' teeth stand, like antique talismans, on President John F. Kennedy's desk in his office at the White House? Why were there another twenty-five or more whales' teeth in the bookshelves and on the tabletops around the room? And on the night before the state funeral of the late President why did his wife put a whale's tooth inscribed with the insignia of his Office, the Seal of the President of the United States, in his coffin, to go with him to his grave in Arlington?

All these teeth were curiously etched with pictures of sailing ships, whaling scenes, notable historic figures, patriotic symbols or famous landmarks. They were highly interesting examples of scrimshaw, carvings on whales' teeth, made by the whalemen in their leisure hours on the long three- and four-year whaling voyages of the nineteenth century. John F. Kennedy, who loved the sea and spent so many of the summers of his life on Nantucket Sound, that rolling cradle of whalemen, was a scrimshaw collector.

The origins of scrimshaw, the breed of men who created it, and a description of the examples of the whaleman's art in Kennedy's collection may be of interest, but why John Kennedy collected scrimshaw is, perhaps, of more import. It is an unusual hobby, but Kennedy was an unusual man. What interested the man tells us a lot about John Kennedy.

Scrimshaw is an enduring record of American whaling, a history interwoven with triumph and tragedy. Whales' teeth are the ivory pages of that record. On some of them the sailors etched vivid scenes of triumphant combat with the leviathans of the deep, the biggest creatures that ever lived on earth. On other teeth they carved weeping willows, flowers in urns and sentiments such as "Forget me not" for memorials to shipmates who had been killed by whales. There are examples of each in President Kennedy's collection. The polished ivory whales' teeth with their pictures of sailing ships and scenes of whaling combat provide an insight into John F. Kennedy's character — a private, intimate, understated side, but it is there. Historians will speculate for years to come about this man of the twentieth century, the problems he faced, the victories and defeats in the days that were allotted to him. They should not dismiss as altogether trivial the story that the various pieces in his scrimshaw collection, these carefully chosen, nostalgic ivories, have to tell us about John Kennedy.

The Whaleman's Art   2

To better understand President Kennedy's deep and abiding interest in scrimshaw, some pertinent background information on this folk art of the whalemen may be helpful.

Original scrimshaw pieces are those pictorial, ornamental and useful things made at sea by whalemen from the teeth and jawbone of the sperm whale, the only large whale with teeth. Baleen, the black, fibrous whalebone from the mouths of toothless whales, narwhal ivory and walrus tusks also provided the whalemen with material for etching and carving. Tropic wood, mother-of-pearl, tortoiseshell, silver or scraps found aboard ship were used for inlay work by the more skillful sailors.

With these materials, whalemen carved all manner of "notions" during their off-duty hours: jagging wheels for crimping pie crusts, adjustable swifts for winding yarn, parasol handles, walking sticks, models of ships and whaleboats, birdcages, boxes, baskets, checkerboards, chessmen, clothespins, rolling pins, needle cases, picture frames, coatracks, footscrapers, bootjacks, knobs, rulers, knives, forks, spoons, children's toys, dollhouse furniture, dominoes, coconut shell dippers, earrings, buttons, cuff links, carved whales of every kind, buggy whips, inkstands, inlaid writing boxes, and whalebone corset busks by the thousands, often elaborately decorated with hearts and flowers. Busks were made from the white jawpan bone of the sperm whale or of black baleen from the whalebone of right whales. They were favorite sentimental gifts to wives or sweethearts. (On the subject of wives and sweethearts, one errant sailor etched a whale's tooth — not in the Kennedy collection — showing a nubile South Sea maiden in a grass skirt on one side and a prim New England lady right out of *Godey's Lady's Book* on the other. These lines are inscribed on the tooth: "To our Wives and Sweethearts, May they never meet.")

The sailor's lexicon of ornament and design was usually found on his own ship: the compass rose, the scrollwork on the ship's stern board or the figurehead, spiral carving in imitation of rope, sailor's knots, anchors, stars, bells, hearts, diamonds, the ship's wheel, and, of course, whales. Occasionally he found a design to suit his purpose in the well-thumbed magazines or books on the ship.

A great deal of scrimshaw work was done by the whalemen in making articles for their own use on shipboard: fids used to open rope strands in splicing, tool handles, logbook stamps, ditty boxes for personal belongings, and numerous other items. Fittings for the ship and the whaleboats, such as blocks and belaying pins, were carved from ivory and whalebone. On some old hookers whale ivory and bone came to be used wherever it could take the place of perishable wood or metal. In *Moby Dick,* Herman Melville painted an unforgettable picture of the old *Pequod,* garnished from stem to stern with scrimshawed fittings:

You may have seen many a quaint craft in your day, for aught I know; — square-toed luggers; mountainous Japanese junks; butter-box galliots, and what not; but take my word for it, you never saw such a rare old craft as this same rare old *Pequod* . . . She was apparelled like any barbaric Ethiopian emperor, his neck heavy with pendants of polished ivory. She was thing of trophies. A cannibal of a craft, tricking herself forth in the chased bones of her enemies. All round, her unpannelled, open bulwarks were garnished like one continuous jaw, with the long sharp teeth of the Sperm Whale, inserted there for pins, to fasten her old hempen thews and tendons to. Those thews ran not through base blocks of landwood, but deftly travelled over sheaves of sea-ivory. Scorning a turnstile wheel at her reverend helm, she sported there a tiller; and that tiller was in one mass, curiously carved from the long narrow jaw of her hereditary foe. The helmsman who steered by that tiller in a tempest, felt like the Tartar, when he holds back his fiery steed by clutching its jaw. A noble craft, but somehow a most melancholy! All noble things are touched with that.

Etched whales' teeth are the most easily recognized examples of scrimshaw. Describing a sailor at work on scrimshaw, the late Clifford Ashley, an able artist and whaling historian, wrote:

> The most familiar fruit of his craft were his graphics on Sperm Whales' teeth. What more natural than to wish to present a distant friend with a trophy of the whale hunt, a huge tooth that, in actual conflict with a whale, had threatened him and now stood a symbol of his success? [1]

A good-sized sperm whale had about forty-two teeth, set in a narrow jawbone perhaps eighteen feet in length. The teeth varied in size and fitted into hard sockets in his head. The top third of the tooth was smooth, but the rest of the tooth below the white gum was rough. The first mate of the whaler was usually in charge of the distribution of teeth and bone for scrimshaw work. The sailors bargained with each other, traded tobacco, or performed menial shipboard tasks for one another in order to gain a big, well-shaped tooth or a choice piece of jawbone.

The natural tooth, pried from the sperm whale's long jawbone, has a ribbed surface which must first be filed down and rubbed smooth. Shark's skin provided an excellent sanding agent. A fresh whale's tooth is softer and more easily worked than an old tooth that has dried out and hardened with age. On the smooth surface the whaleman carefully penciled and then carved with his knife point pictures of his ship and scenes of whaling combat. The etched lines were then made visible by filling them with black India ink, or greasy soot from the try-pots. Tobacco juice also made an effective coloring agent. Dyes and paint were used if additional color was desired. When this dried, the surface was given a final polishing. Ashes from the fire under the try-pots and elbow grease gave the scrimshawed tooth its final luster.

The indispensable tool of scrimshaw was the sailor's jackknife. With it he drew and carved, often more easily than he could write. Files, saws, planes and a turning lathe could usually be found at the cooper's bench. Ashley stated that a great deal of fine turning was actually simulated with a file, and much of the pattern in scrimshaw work that resembles scroll sawing was also file work. Holes were drilled with gimlets made of nails. The countersinking for tortoiseshell, silver, and mother-of-pearl inlay was scraped out with a knife, helped sometimes with a chisel.

There is a passage in *Moby Dick* in which Melville describes scrimshaw work (or "skrimshandering," as Melville called it in the Golden Age of Whaling), and then he goes on to give us an expert's critique on the sailor-savages who created a barbaric art in their etching and carving on whale ivory:

Throughout the Pacific, and also in Nantucket and New Bedford and Sag Harbor, you will come across lively sketches of whales and whaling scenes, graven by the fishermen themselves on Sperm Whale-teeth, or ladies' busks wrought out of the right whale-bone, and other like skrimshander articles, as the whalemen call the numerous little ingenious contrivances they elaborately carve out of the rough material, in their hours of ocean leisure. Some of them have little boxes of dentistical-looking implements, specially intended for the skrimshandering business. But, in general, they toil with their jack-knives alone; and with that omnipotent tool of the sailor, they will turn out anything you please, in the way of a mariner's fancy.

Long exile from Christendom and civilization inevitably restores a man to that condition in which God placed him, i.e., what is called savagery. Your true whale hunter is as much a savage as an Iroquois. I myself am a savage, owing no allegiance but to the King of the Cannibals; and ready at any moment to rebel against him.

Now, one of the peculiar characteristics of the savage in his domestic hours, is his wonderful patience of industry. An ancient Hawaiian war-club or spear-paddle, in its full multiplicity and elaboration of carving, is as great a trophy of human perseverance as a Latin lexicon. For, with but a bit of broken sea-shell or a shark's tooth, that miraculous intricacy of wooden net-work has been achieved; and it has cost steady years of steady application.

As with the Hawaiian savage, so with the white sailor-savage. With the same marvelous patience, and with the same single shark's tooth, of his one poor jack-knife, he will carve you a bit of bone sculpture, not quite as work-manlike, but as closely packed in its maziness of design as the Greek savage, Achilles's shield; and full of barbaric spirit and suggestiveness as the prints of that fine old Dutch savage, Albrecht Dürer.

Melville's definition of scrimshaw as a savage art is borne out by Joseph Hart in his book *Miriam Coffin*. He describes the elaborate, painstaking work, the wild concept and design that went into the scrimshaw walking stick of Jethro Coffin: "It was wrought into diamonds and ridges, and squares and oblongs, like the war clubs of the South Sea Islanders, and surmounted by the head of a grinning Sea Lion, with a straight black pin of polished whalebone driven through his ears."[2]

Scrimshaw is above all a masculine art. Even though many articles of scrimshaw were made for sentimental gifts, wrought with tender affection for loved ones at home, the virile, barbaric feeling comes through. Just as a painting tells us something about the painter, so the pagan design and execution that went into scrimshaw work reflected the temperament of the sailor-savage.

If scrimshaw is a most masculine art, there are some known exceptions to the rule. A few of the whaling wives who accompanied their captain-husbands on long voyages tried their feminine hands at scrimshaw. At remote Desolation Island in the Indian Ocean in 1878, Mrs. Israel Morey, wife of the master of the ship *Catawha,* made a whalebone spool holder as a gift to the wife of another captain back on Nantucket. Mrs. Sallie Smith, who put to sea with her husband in the bark *Ohio* in 1875, kept a diary in which she mentioned helping Captain Smith make a box of bone. Captain Frederick Smith was an expert at scrimshaw. He built himself a rare scrimshaw turning lathe of whalebone mounted on wood, which he used during the *Ohio*'s whaling voyage in the South Seas. There is also an entry in the log of the bark *Benjamin Cummings* on New Year's Day, 1858, which recorded that "Captain Jenkins and wife and all hands scrimshoring."[3]

Ashley estimated that in the seventy or eighty years of real Yankee whaling, some twenty thousand whalemen, year in and year out, spent their leisure time in scrimshawing every conceivable kind of object. If each whaleman made only one piece of scrimshaw a year, the figure would come to around one million six hundred thousand examples of the whaleman's art. Many sailors, however, were prolific producers

14

This whale's tooth began the Kennedy scrimshaw collection. Mrs. Kennedy gave it to her husband while he was still a Senator from the Bay State. The full-rigged ship etched on sea ivory stirred Kennedy's collector's interest in whaling scrimshaw, particularly in sailing ships incised on whales' teeth. The President's new, avid interest in scrimshaw helped simplify the wifely problem of what to give her husband at Christmas or birthdays. In his White House office this gift from Mrs. Kennedy always held the front-center position on the President's desk.

of scrimshawed items, and it might be safe to estimate the total production of genuine whaling scrimshaw at nearer three million pieces. Where has it all gone?

Scrimshaw, like gold, is where you find it. A fine piece may turn up in a junk shop in Ohio or at a rummage sale in Iowa. Retired whalemen not infrequently migrated to the rich farmlands of upper New York State or the fertile areas of the Western Reserve. Having gained a competence at whaling, they swallowed the anchor and went West to pioneer in new fields. They took with them their household lares and penates.

President Kennedy acquired a liking for scrimshaw before he entered the White House when Mrs. Kennedy, knowing his love of naval Americana, gave him a whale's tooth on which had been etched an American ship under full sail. This seems to have set a pattern, for his interest first centered on whales' teeth carrying pictures of sailing ships. Later, he began to add teeth and walrus tusks with pictures of noted historical figures to his growing collection.

There were thirty-seven pieces of scrimshaw in the President's collection, consisting of thirty-four etched teeth and three decorated walrus tusks. All the pieces were displayed in his White House office. His desk was liberally covered with whales' teeth. The bookshelves and tabletops held other examples, and Evelyn Lincoln, the President's secretary, said that it became something of a problem deciding where to place new scrimshaw pieces as the collection grew. The walls were hung with paintings of historic American naval engagements and other memorabilia of the sea that Kennedy loved. There was an aura of history, past and present, in that room.

Scrimshawed portraits of the Great Elector of Saxony and Christian VI, King of Norway, mounted on tooled leather bases served as bookends in the recessed shelves near the President's desk. They are almost certainly of foreign origin and etched with the professional touch of a trained engraver. The portrait of Alexander Hamilton on the shelf below is pure American whaleman's folk art, copied as well as he could do it from an engraving. Encased in glass, a model of PT 109 rests on the bottom shelf.

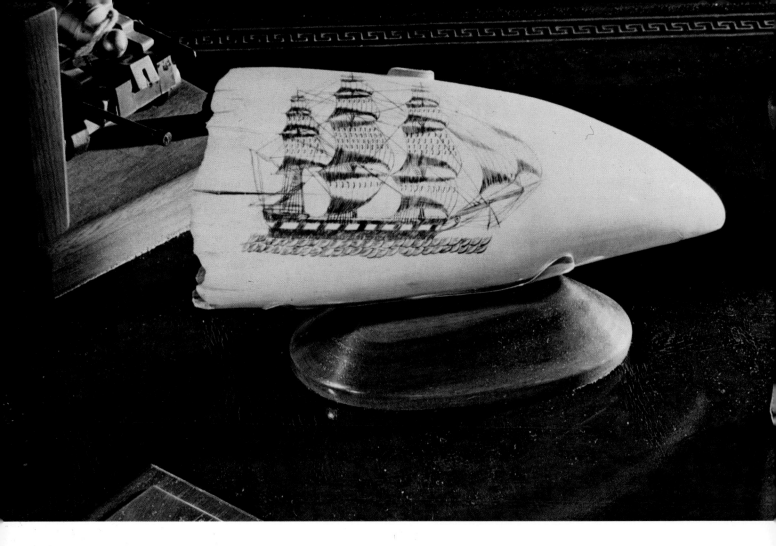

When the Kennedys were at their home on the Cape, the President liked to do a little browsing around, looking for scrimshawed whales' teeth. He picked up several pieces from dealers in antiques of a nautical nature. But because of the heavy demands on his time, so much of which had to be spent in Washington, Kennedy was helped by his close friends and members of his family in the formation of the collection.

A whale's tooth with the frigate running before the wind, her sails billowing out as she cuts through the sea at perhaps twelve to fourteen knots, came to President Kennedy as a gift from LeMoyne Billings, his roommate at Choate and his lifelong friend. On a wood and silver mount it sat on the left side of Kennedy's desk. On the back of the whale's tooth there is a picture of a lady with a tiny parasol. It is quite primitive and not done with that sureness and knowledge the sailor showed in etching the sailing ship. Perhaps the artist copied the figure from a magazine, but it would not seem to have been traced or transferred. Behind it to the left in the photograph may be seen part of a bookend with a replica of a cannon from the *Constitution* mounted on a wooden base. In the foreground is J.F.K.'s own memento of the Cuban missile crisis of October, 1962. President Ken-

nedy had a small number of these polished metal plaques made up with the initials of each of his close advisers during those touch-and-go days which are highlighted on the calendar.

LeMoyne Billings shared the President's interest in scrimshaw, and he was of substantial help to Kennedy in the building of his collection. Billings kept in touch with dealers who specialized in nautical items, and he arranged for them to send scrimshaw pieces to Kennedy for his consideration.

He enlisted the help of George Wintress, an officer in The Seamen's Bank for Savings whose special interest is in the great collection of scrimshaw, marine paintings and ship models owned and displayed by that nautically oriented institution. Dealers bring their new acquisitions to such known collectors.

Wintress was able to forward to the White House a number of whales' teeth scrimshawed with the special kind of subject matter that would interest Kennedy. A particularly good whale's tooth, etched with the portrait of Captain William Henry Allen, was sent to Mrs. Kennedy, who wished to give her husband a present for his collection.

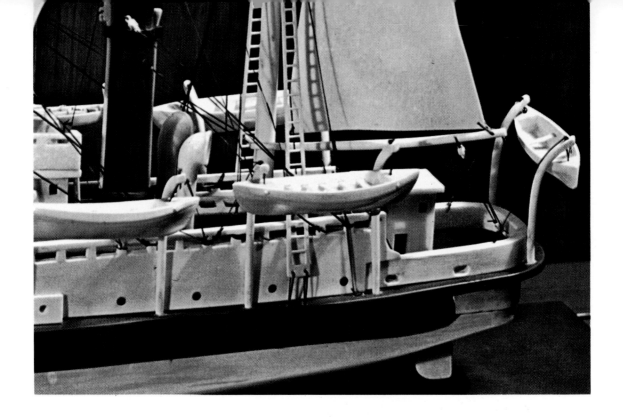

Some of the earliest pieces which Kennedy acquired through
Wintress were very reasonably priced. One such whale's tooth, inscribed with a sailing ship, the President presented to Prime Minister
Harold Macmillan when he visited the White House. The unusual gift
evidently made a hit, and Kennedy asked Wintress to send a supply
to be kept on hand for such occasions. Mr. Wintress regretfully had
to inform the President that suitably scrimshawed whales' teeth were
rare, and bargains were becoming even more rare. Wintress was instrumental in providing President Kennedy with the ship model of
the U.S.S. *Constitution* which he presented to Premier Khrushchev
at their Vienna conference. The astute Russians were aware of Kennedy's interest in scrimshaw, and Khrushchev's gift to the President
was a handsome walrus ivory and whalebone model of an American
sail-and-steam bark-rigged whaler of the type that frequented the
Arctic whaling grounds off Siberia. Khrushchev's gift was accompanied by a friendly note:

June 15, 1961

Dear Mr. President:

In Vienna you told me you are fond of collecting models of vessels. It is
with pleasure that I am sending you a model of an American whaler of which
I told you during one of our conversations. This model, made of walrus tusk
and whalebone, was carved from memory by a talented, self-taught Chuktchi
craftsman. Such sail-steam vessels were in use in the end of the nineteenth
century in the Chuktchi Sea for whale-fishing, and they would visit Russian
harbors. I will be glad if the model of this vessel becomes part of your
collection . . . [4]

20

LeMoyne Billings recalls that the President was very definite about what he wanted and what he wanted to pay. Pieces were sent to him on approval; if they didn't suit his taste, or if the price seemed too high, back they went. Kennedy was willing to pay a fair price for desirable scrimshaw, but he did not propose to build up a quick collection by all-out spending. Several early acquisitions were picked up at real bargain prices, and perhaps at first this influenced Kennedy when it came to getting out his checkbook; some of the last and finest whales' teeth were picked up at an auction of scrimshaw at Parke-Bernet in October 1963, when agents for the President paid the going market price for scrimshaw.

In connection with President Kennedy's collecting habits, it is interesting to recall Kennedy's remarks at the opening of an exhibit of President Franklin D. Roosevelt's naval prints in June, 1962, at the National Archives Building in Washington. The exhibit of Roosevelt's prints was President Kennedy's own idea, and he asked the great naval historian Admiral Samuel Eliot Morison to make a selection from the vast collection at Hyde Park.

Kennedy's short, graceful speech at the opening of the exhibit tells us a good deal about both of those sea-loving Presidents, revealing their methods in developing their collections, and his remarks deserve to be read in President Kennedy's own words:

I want to express the appreciation, I know, of all of us to the Archives for the devoted work of those who have made this exhibit possible.

About a year ago, I read an article in the *New York Times* about the extraordinary collection of naval prints which was referred to as the largest and best known in this country. Even though I have been interested in the sea from my earliest boyhood, I had not been aware of what President Roosevelt had done in this field.

I think all of us were very familiar with the stamp collection. But the fact that he had — in addition to having one of the finest stamp collections in the United States if not in the world, that he also had — in spite of having some other interests in his life, the most unusual collection of naval prints indicates an extraordinary versatility as well as vitality to which he brought everything that he did. So that I thought it would be very appropriate that the best of these pictures should come to Washington and be exhibited. And I hope that after the exhibition is completed here it can go on to other parts of the country so that other Americans can see it.

It serves two very useful purposes. First, it tells us more about a very important part of our lives — our lives at sea. We think of ourselves, I think, as land animals in a sense, but we really look to the sea — the Atlantic and the Pacific — which have defended us and have secured us and have enriched us.

Our naval history is one of the most exciting threads that runs throughout the long history of our country, and the combination of the Navy and the Maritime and the extraordinary men who served and who gave it life and thrust and thesis deserves to be recorded.

So I think this exhibit will enrich all of those who look east and west from our seashore.

In addition, I think it tells us something about one of our most distinguished Presidents. He did not spend very much money on this collection. He looked for bargains. His descent was Dutch and frugal. He did not merely buy other collectors' exhibits, but instead he went over catalogues for long periods of time. Mr. Louis Howe represented him and went to a number of places and secured pictures and some extraordinary bargains. In 1938–1939 he felt that the prices were getting too high, and his collection began to taper off. So this was not a question of putting large financial resources into buying it the easy way, but instead, day after day, year after year it was built up, and now it is extraordinary.

In order to make this exhibit truly meaningful, we asked our great historian,

Admiral Morison, if he would be kind enough, with the cooperation of the Government people here and the Librarian at Hyde Park, to pick the pictures which should be exhibited. Admiral Morison, who has been so generous to the Navy and really to all of us who are interested in the Navy, agreed to do so; and he is here today. And we are very indebted to him for participating in this exhibit.

We hope that this opening today, attended as it is by the family and old friends of President Roosevelt — that we will be the first of a great number of Americans who will touch, through this exhibit, not only the life of President Roosevelt but also the old Navy. [5]

If President Roosevelt was Dutch and frugal in his print collecting, President Kennedy could show a real New England thrift when it came to buying scrimshaw.

Until 1960, most antique dealers didn't know what scrimshaw was. (This, of course, does not include dealers on Cape Cod or other specialists in nautical memorabilia.) So in many shops a discerning collector could browse, expressing an interest in anything in ivory, boxes, canes, carvings or what all, and walk out with a bargain. There are stories of dealers and collectors who picked up trunkloads and barrels of scrimshaw many years ago for figures like ten dollars!

When it became known that President Kennedy was a scrimshaw collector, prices shot up. Dealers now recognize a scrimshawed whale's tooth and they ask incredible prices for mediocre examples, of which there are many. Modern production line copies of scrimshaw sell for more than genuine old-time pieces brought not many years ago. Today's bargains, if there are any, are to be found in the less easily recognized scrimshaw items. A collector's judgment and taste can be formed by studying the great collections in the New Bedford, Mystic and other whaling museums. The knowledge so obtained may still gain the collector a bargain.

These two small whales' teeth appear to be modern scrimshaw which came to President Kennedy as a gift. The tooth on the left was exhibited with other Kennedy memorabilia on a tour in behalf of the Kennedy Library. It is now missing. The remaining small tooth is, however, almost a duplicate.

Men of the Stone Age and the Bronze Age made useful objects of bone and ivory, and so it may be contended that the origin of whaling scrimshaw really dates back beyond the dawn of recorded history. When American whalemen began fashioning useful and ornamental articles from whale ivory and bone, they merely substituted that choice, durable material for the wood they had previously used in whittling various and sundry articles while at sea.

The catching of whales goes back to prehistoric times. There are neolithic rock carvings of whaling in Norway which were done in 6000 B.C. Wherever there were whales, primitive man found ways to take them. Whales' rib bones were used in building boats and framing rude huts. Whale ivory, walrus tusks and the strange spiral tooth of the narwhal, sometimes eight to ten feet long, were used in the carving of figures and useful articles in very ancient times and in all parts of the world. The Phoenicians, the Chinese and the Japanese, the Vikings, the Basques and the Irish used sea ivory in carving all sorts of objects, from sword hilts to magic amulets.

Herman Melville's vast research of ancient sources in the writing of *Moby Dick* produces this quote from "Octher's verbal narrative taken down from his mouth by King Alfred, A.D. 890":

He visited this country also with a view of catching horsewhales [walrus], which had bones of very great value for their teeth, of which he brought some to the king.

In 1831, seventy-eight chessmen, carved out of walrus ivory, were found in a sandbank at Vig, in the Isle of Lewis, Outer Hebrides. These chess pieces, enough to form seven or eight sets, are thought to belong to the late eleventh or twelfth century. Perhaps they came there when some Norse trading vessel was wrecked in a storm.

In the British Museum there is another lot of chessmen, found at Witchampton Manor, Dorset. The Witchampton pieces are of whalebone, carved in a simpler style than the Isle of Lewis chessmen, and it has been suggested that they date somewhere between the tenth and twelfth century.

Chrétien de Troyes, in the late part of the twelfth century, wrote a poem with a reference to a set of magic chessmen made of ivory which had been carved on the banks of the Thames in London. In the fourteenth and fifteenth centuries, to play a good game of chess was an essential part of the cultural education of men and women alike.

In old Japan, netsukes were the little carved pieces used to fasten or catch the drawstrings of the bags that were carried in lieu of pockets. Whale, walrus and narwhal ivory were often the materials chosen by the craftsman. A narwhal netsuke served a dual purpose. In addition to its use as a fastener, the narwhal netsuke had a medical function. The long spiral unicorn tooth of the narwhal was thought to have special medicinal properties by both the Chinese and the Japanese. The carved piece of unicorn ivory was used for netsuke at ordinary times, and when the wearer was attacked by fever, scrapings from the netsuke were swallowed to allay the fever. It is said that since narwhal is hard to distinguish from other ivories, the spot where the cord is fastened was left with a crust, and no carving was done there, so that the material might be recognized as narwhal ivory; and scrapings could be taken from it without affecting the general design. It was thought that scrapings of narwhal ivory, taken internally, would cause thorns or splinters in the skin to come out.

It was once believed, too, that narwhal ivory could be used to detect poison in wine or food. Contact with any poisonous substance was supposed to discolor the ivory.

In certain South Sea Islands, whales' teeth were, and still are, considered to be of as great value as any diamonds ever dug from the Kimberley fields. Queen Salote, of the Tonga Islands, came from the South Pacific to the Coronation of Queen Elizabeth II, bearing a gift of polished whales' teeth to bring the new Queen happiness and good fortune in her reign.

In the age of Yankee whaling it was not uncommon for a harpooneer to wear a small whale's tooth as a sort of fetish or good luck piece on a necklace of intricately knotted twine.

The earliest American mention this writer has been able to find of carving on whale ivory, more than a century before such work was called scrimshaw, is a reference to a "cane with its handle carved from a whale's tooth," carried by Samuel Mulford, of East Hampton, Long Island, in 1704. [6]

Samuel Mulford was the head of the first whaling company in America, established by the settlers on the tip of Long Island. As was usually the case, drift whales, found floating dead on the surface, and stranded whales were first taken. Then the early colonists began shore whaling in small boats, capturing whales that appeared regularly off Long Island from December to April.

It is sometimes difficult to judge whether an article made of whale ivory, walrus tusk or narwhal ivory was actually made at sea and hence entitled to be called genuine scrimshaw. If the piece is carved or embellished with designs of a nautical nature, it may be safe to assume it is whaling scrimshaw. But many old items made of whale or walrus ivory were not made on shipboard. William King, for example, advertised his ivory-turning trade in the *Salem Mercury* of July 21, 1789, in which he offered: "genteel canes and Riding Sticks, Fifes, Dice and Dice Boxes, Backgammon Boards and Men, Chess ditto, Billiard Balls, Ivory and Bone Syringes, Shaving Boxes, and any other turned work in ivory, bone, horn, turtle-shell, wood, etc. — a good price given for Ivory and Sea Cow [walrus] teeth."

Sperm whales, whose teeth and jawbones supplied the material for scrimshaw, traveled all over the world, although they were usually found in temperate waters, particularly in the Pacific Ocean. The sperm whale's coat of blubber is not as thick as the blubber of the right whales, humpback whales and the bowhead whales which inhabit the Arctic waters. Sperm whales, however, were found occasionally in the far north. There is an interesting entry in the logbook of the *John Bunyan,* Captain Allan, which would indicate the taking of a sperm whale on the coast of Greenland on July 20, 18 —"[7]

Broke out meat and whales' teeth and divided them among all hands. Myself and a few other at the vice [sic] bench cleaning our whales teeth . . . employed splitting bone and scraping gum off the ends of it.

Another evidence of sperm whales in the Arctic Ocean is found in the *Narrative of the Second Arctic Expedition 1864–1869* by Charles F. Hall. Hall, with financial support from old whaling families in New London, Connecticut, set out alone to try to discover what happened to Sir John Franklin's ill-fated expedition which was lost in an attempt to discover the Northwest Passage. Hall lived in winter quarters with the Innuits at Repulse Bay. On one of his trips in search of evidence of Franklin's expedition he reported:

> On the island a native sledge was found, made entirely of the jawbone of a whale. It was very heavy. The runners were twelve feet long, ten inches deep, and one and a half inches thick, and were shod with the same bone; the cross-bars measured twenty inches. Ou-e-la said that it belongs to the father of I-vit-chuck. [8]

This big bone sledge, of course, was not Yankee whaling scrimshaw, but it is certainly the biggest article of whalebone this writer has ever heard of! The Innuit father of I-vit-chuck is to be saluted for the enterprise and imagination he showed. Perhaps the sledge still sits on that lonely island in the north, waiting for a collector to come along.

The earliest writer to discuss American scrimshaw in any detail was J. Hector St. John de Crèvecoeur in his *Letters from an American Farmer,* first published in 1782. Crèvecoeur visited Nantucket and Martha's Vineyard in the early 1770's, and he left a fascinating account of the inhabitants of those sister islands in the sea and the business of whaling as it was carried on in the early days. He described scrimshaw before there was even a name for it; and he would seem to be the first to disclose its raison d'etre, the Puritan ethic, that desire to be doing something useful to while away the long hours at sea:

> Idleness is the most heinous sin that can be committed in Nantucket: an idle man would soon be pointed out as an object of compassion: for idleness is considered as another word for want and hunger. This principle is so thor-

oughly well understood, and it is become so universal, so prevailing a prejudice, that literally speaking, they are never idle. Even if they go to the marketplace, which is (if I may be allowed the expression) the coffee-house of the town, either to transact business, or to converse with friends, they always have a piece of cedar in their hands, and while they are talking, they will, as it were instinctively, employ themselves in converting it to something useful, either in making bungs or spoyls for their oil casks, or other useful articles. I must confess, that I have never seen more ingenuity in the use of the knife; thus the most idle moments of their lives become usefully employed. In the many hours of leisure which their long cruises afford them, they cut and carve a variety of boxes and pretty toys, in wood, adapted to different uses; which they bring home as testimonies of remembrance to their wives and sweethearts. They have showed me a variety of little bowls and other implements, executed cooper-wise, with the greatest neatness and elegance. You will be pleased to remember they are all brought up to the trade of coopers, be their future intentions or fortunes what they may; therefore almost every man in this island has always two knives in his pocket, one much larger than the other; and though they hold everything that is called *fashion* in the utmost contempt, yet they are as difficult to please, and as extravagant in the choice and price of their knives, as any young buck in Boston would be about his hat, buckles, or coat. [9]

Wood was the usual material employed by the whalemen for scrimshaw work in those early days which St. John de Crèvecoeur recalls. Although sperm whales were captured from time to time, it was not until the whalemen entered the Pacific and took sperm whales in great numbers that the more durable ivory teeth and pan bone became the favored material. The jackknife continued to be the indispensable tool, along with the sail needle and the file.

There is very little literature written by the whalemen themselves on the subject of scrimshaw. Occasionally, in diaries or letters, there were descriptions of ''skrimshandering'' work in progress. From some of these sources actual pieces have been identified and dated. Mention of scrimshawing is made in many of the old whaleship log-books, usually brief entries to the effect that there was nothing to do, no whales to catch, and all hands were employed scrimshawing. Whaleships often cruised for weeks and even months without sighting a whale. And for thirty or more men cooped up in the narrow confines of the ship, year in and year out, scrimshaw work provided the answer to boredom and monotony.

On the subject of the monotonous inactivity that was an inevitable part of whaling, there is a passage from Captain William M. Davis's Journal and quoted in his book *Nimrod of the Sea, or the American Whaleman:*

Jan. 23. The sky is clear, with fresh winds. We are now regularly cruising with not enough to do to keep a man off a growl. As this habit cankers the soul, I prefer to scrimshone. Odd minutes are now employed in the rigging of a little brig. She is carved from a piece of beautiful California cedar, hollowed out neatly, and sheathed in planks of black whalebone, the port streak being of white bone from the sperm whale jaw. The masts and spars are of the same material. The blocks are of pearl-shell ground and polished, and it is my intention, as time is nothing, to give her every appointment of a brig above deck. Her shrouds are now neatly ratlined up to the top-gallant head, and some of her yards are across. [10]

The origin of the word scrimshaw has been a matter of hazy speculation for many years. Much evidence, however, leads to the conclusion that scrimshaw, or an earlier version, skrimshander, was nineteenth century sailors' slang very close in meaning to our twentieth century slang word, boondoggle (defined by Webster as: "any unnecessary and wasteful project; to engage in boondoggles; derogatorily, to engage in useless or frivolous occupations'').

Scrimshaw is the final spelling of the word. Older versions included scrimshan, scrimshon, squimshon, scrimshorn, schrimsha, and skrimshander. These variations are taken from books on whaling, ships' logs and letters the whalemen wrote. Melville spelled it ''skrimshandering'' in *Moby Dick.* A shand, according to Webster, is a worthless person.

Edouard A. Stackpole, in his excellent book *Scrimshaw at Mystic Seaport,* states that the word would appear to come from the Dutch *skrimshander,* meaning one who indulges too much in lying around, or a lazy fellow.

The *Oxford English Dictionary* defines ''scrimshank'' as British slang meaning to shirk one's duty. It goes on to quote a line from the *Pilot,* October 17, 1903, ''We all know you are due for a long scrimshank next month.'' In the British army a scrimshanker is a soldier who dodges work.

In *The Whale and His Captors,* an account of his voyage on the *Commodore Preble,* published in 1850, Rev. Henry T. Cheever wrote:

Mux and skimshander are the general names by which they express the way in which the whalemen busy themselves when making passages, and in the intervals of taking whales. [11]

To ''mux'' is to mess up, or botch a job, according to Webster. ''Mux and skimshander'' was the whaleman's own self-derogatory way of referring to the messing around, botching and boondoggling, the work they did on whale ivory to kill time.

Back in 1887, James Templeman Brown, a fine old whaling historian, gave a page or two to the subject of scrimshaw in which he stated that the whale fisherman often became so engrossed in "scrimshawing" as to cause him to *neglect his duties*. [12] Brown thought the word came in corrupt form from the Nantucket Indian tongue. This theory has long since been discounted. Brown wrote at a time when whaling was still a fairly active business, and he talked with many whalemen. It might be surmised that the earliest downgrading meaning of the word had been succeeded by the present definition: articles of bone and ivory made for themselves by the whalemen in their leisure hours at sea.

Obed Macy in his *History of Nantucket* and Alexander Starbuck in the *History of the American Whale Fishery* both apparently felt that scrimshaw was too trivial a pastime to merit discussion. The whalemen were out there on business, and the business was to catch whales.

The whaleman's interest in scrimshaw and the leisure-hour days, weeks, and months devoted to scrimshaw projects was once a matter of hot debate among shipowners, not a few of whom felt that too great interest in scrimshaw was harmful to the success of voyages. Ashley wrote that certain captains forbade scrimshaw altogether. On some ships its practice was permitted only in the forecastle. Any sailor who brought his work up on deck was liable to have it confiscated.

It would seem fairly conclusive that the original word skrimshander, scrimshaw, or whatever, was not highly complimentary whalers' slang for the work they did on whales' teeth and bone to kill time. But scrimshawing gave them an interest, a means of expressing

34

This handsomely executed and tinted pair of whales' teeth was bought at auction in 1963. It may be noted that the ships are almost identically drawn, but the ship on the left flies the broad, swallow-tailed pennant of a commodore at her masthead, and guns project from her open ports. The ship on the right flies the long pennant, or whip, carried by a government vessel in commission, and her gunports are closed. The stylized handling of the sea is the same on each tooth, but the ornamentation of flags and graceful leafy borders differs.

themselves. What they may have regarded as of little accoun , a later generation has come to admire and appreciate as a not insignificant contribution to American art and whaling history.

John Kennedy's interest in scrimshaw was highly specialized. Of all the wide range of scrimshaw items made by the sailors, Kennedy selected only teeth or walrus tusks with pictures of whaleships, sailing ships of the old Navy, historic American landmarks, patriotic symbols, or famous men. Any pieces in the collection that did not fit in with Kennedy's own limitations may be presumed to have come as gifts that could not be turned down. What, then, was it that interested John Kennedy in the specific examples of scrimshaw he chose for his collection? What made those scrimshawed whales' teeth important enough to the President of the United States to take over the top of his desk in the White House?

Scrimshaw and Salt Water   3

. . . beaches, surf, tranquil salt water, peace, sunlight, color, sounds of nature, harmonies of sky and water, blueberries, lobsters, hills, woods, sound sleep and a return to youth . . .
— HENRY BEETLE HOUGH, *The Vineyard Gazette*

As a boy growing up in the long summers on Cape Cod, you take those things pretty much for granted, but all the while salt spray, wild roses, skinny-dipping at night, quahog chowder, sailing, going barefoot, these things are quietly at work to give you a love for the sea and the seashore through all your days.

There is even a certain somber beauty in a three-day northeaster, when people take their children to the exposed beaches where the storm-driven surf comes thundering in, breaking and running far up on the beach, trying to catch the squealing kids as they race to get out of the way.

On quiet, foggy days houses become gray, ghostly shadows, and far-off foghorns moan. A child remembers these things, along with all the bright, sunny days.

Most people retain an affection for the place where they were brought up, where they spent the happy hours of childhood. For some, it is the mountains or the lakes. For John Kennedy it was the sea and the seashore. To him the Cape was home.

The family had lived in Brookline, in New York's Riverdale, in Bronxville, and later in Washington and London, but when Joseph P. Kennedy bought the big house by the sea in Hyannis Port it was for keeps, and the Kennedy children knew that from then on, the home at the Cape was where their roots really were. The house with the big lawn and the beach, where the younger ones could collect pebbles, shells and frosty bits of sea glass, gave them a feeling of permanence and security. And as they grew up, married and started families of their own, the number of houses in the famous compound has grown. Now it is a place where grandchildren repeat the age-old process of growing up to love the sea and the Cape in the sparkling morning of life.

Jack Kennedy was twelve years old in 1929, when his father bought the rambling, ten-bedroom house at Hyannis Port. He and his older brother Joe learned to swim and sail in the summer waters of Nantucket Sound. As his father said, "Joe and Jack were out in sailboats here at Hyannis Port when they were so small you couldn't see their heads. It looked from the shore as if the boats were empty."

At first they were told to stay inside the breakwater that formed a sheltered harbor in front of the house. It was an ideal place to learn the business of sailing, with plenty of people around to come to the rescue in case help was needed. Once they proved that they knew how to handle a boat, they were allowed to sail outside on Nantucket Sound. It was not long before Jack Kennedy was competing as a young racing skipper in the various sailing regattas on the Cape and at the old whaling ports of Nantucket and Edgartown, on Martha's Vineyard.

So Jack Kennedy joined the unending ranks of youngsters who learned the ways of the sea at an early age in sailing the waters of Nantucket Sound. Far back in the early 1770's, Hector St. John de Crèvecoeur described how boys learned to sail in its ideal waters:

Those children born by the sea-side, hearing the roaring of its waves as soon as they are able to listen; it is the first noise with which they become acquainted, and by plunging into it they acquire that boldness, that presence of mind and dexterity, which makes them ever after such expert seamen . . . They often cross the sea to go to the main, and learn even in those short voyages to qualify themselves for longer and more dangerous ones; they are therefore deservedly conspicuous for their maritime knowledge and experience all over the continent. [1]

Crèvecoeur's observation was made almost two centuries ago, but it applies as validly today to the youngsters who sail the waters of Nantucket Sound. It has always been a nursery of seamen — for the whaleman of long ago and for the PT boat skipper of World War II.

Joe Kennedy, the older brother, was a natural athlete, solid and husky, while Jack was the lanky type who had to make up for the weight handicap by sheer, driving grit. He did well enough in swimming, and he made the Harvard junior varsity football team, but it was in sailing that he really scored. In the 1936 Atlantic Coast Championships he represented Nantucket Sound, sailing his Star Class boat, *Flash II*. In 1938 he was a member of the Harvard Intercollegiate Championship sailing crew, along with his brother Joe. And in that same year Jack Kennedy represented Harvard in the annual competition at Annapolis for the Macmillan Cup. Competing against entries from other Ivy League colleges, the Coast Guard Academy and the Naval Academy, Kennedy won the Cup for Harvard. The Macmillan Cup Competition brings together the very best college racing skippers each year. (Bus Mosbacher and Bob Bavier were both former winners in this competition who went on to skipper America's Cup Defenders: Mosbacher with *Weatherly* in 1962, and Bavier on *Constellation* in the 1964 Cup Races.) In 1938 Jack Kennedy could hold his own on the water in any racing company. Those who crewed for him from time to time, LeMoyne Billings, his roommate at Choate, and Torbert Macdonald, his Harvard roommate, say that when it came to sailing a race, Jack Kennedy was all business, no nonsense. He always raced to win, a habit the father inculcated in the Kennedy boys at an early age.

As a boy growing up in Hyannis Port, Jack Kennedy read everything he could find that dealt with Cape Cod and the sea; stories by Joseph C. Lincoln that depicted so well the characteristics of old Cape Codders; Henry Thoreau, who loved its seagirt sands and described the Cape as "the bare and bended arm of Massachusetts"; and, of course, any books that had to do with the history of the Cape, the early settlers, stories of pirates, stories about the Cape during the American Revolution, the War of 1812, and the Age of Whaling. History becomes very real when you live right where it once happened. You see the old houses of the whalemen, landmarks and relics, and the historic past comes alive.

The Indians were the first American whalemen, and their method of going out in many canoes, using bone harpoons fastened to ropes made of bark, the use of logs or inflated skins as floats, and shooting arrows until the whale was killed, was described by an early English explorer and navigator, Captain George Waymouth, in 1605.

Great numbers of whales all along the New England coast were reported by the earliest writers. The master and the mate of the *Mayflower*, carrying the Pilgrims to Plymouth, saw many whales in Cape Cod Bay, that great protected "harbor wherein a thousand sail of ships may ride safely." [2]

The American whale fishery began when the first settlers at Plymouth and Cape Cod found drift and stranded whales along the beaches. This led to shore whaling in small boats.

Learning from the Indians how to take whales along the shore and with their improved iron harpoons, long lances and other whaling gear, the Cape Codders soon became proficient whalemen; so able, indeed, that in 1690 the Nantucketers invited Ichabod Paddock, an

experienced Cape Cod whale hunter, to settle on their island and teach them the business of whaling. Paddock moved to Nantucket with his family, and the Cape Cod man may be said to have fathered the whale fishery at Nantucket.

The Cape and the islands on Nantucket Sound where Kennedy sailed are redolent with whaling history, a history usually involving men of courage, and it would be difficult to grow up there without being imbued with an awareness of their maritime traditions.

Among the scrimshawed whales' teeth in President Kennedy's collection there is one etched with a typical scene of whaling combat. It is a scene that was repeated thousands and thousands of times in bygone days: the taking of a whale on the ocean and recording the picture on a scrimshawed whale's tooth.

Two whaleboats, oars apeak, are fast to a big black monster that has tossed his mighty flukes high in the air. A third whaleboat stands by, ready to help if needed. The whaleship follows, awaiting the outcome, with a masthead lookout reporting the course of the combat to the ship keepers left on board while the boats are away. On the horizon mountainous peaks loom up, resembling the Azores. The signal flag atop the mainmast indicates that whales are up. The ship is etched with all the authority and knowledge of a real whaleman. The lines, the sails, the rigging of the ship are right.

Growing up as a boy on Cape Cod, sailing and swimming in Nantucket Sound, coming to know in the plastic years of his youth the traditions and the whaling heritage of the Cape and those fabled islands, Nantucket and Martha's Vineyard — these things helped to give John F. Kennedy his love of the sea and an affectionate regard, an admiration and respect for the old-time breed of whalemen who contributed so much to our maritime heritage.

As President, he returned again and again to his home at the seashore. Theodore Sorensen, who accompanied Kennedy to the Cape so many times, said that with the continual burden of the Presidency, "a break in the routines helped prevent them from breaking him." Kennedy felt it best for his family life and his personal outlook to get away from the White House, when he could, for a minimum twenty-four hours on a weekend, and for entire weekends and occasional longer holidays in the summer; and sometimes in the hazy Indian summer that lingers so long on the Cape, he returned to Hyannis Port. Sorensen wrote:

> When at the seaside, he took long walks and swims, played with his children in the sand, devoured light as well as heavy reading and went boating with his father and family . . . He relaxed best of all on the water. Although he sailed less frequently than he had in his younger days . . . he loved the sea as he had since childhood . . . On board either the family or Presidential cruiser, the President read history or biography or fiction, chatted with family and friends, waved at passing boats, watched local sailing races and enjoyed the distance between himself and the Secret Service. [3]

The *Honey Fitz,* the Presidential cruiser which had been the *Barbara Ann* in the Eisenhower years, gave President Kennedy many happy hours. She was used to great advantage in the informal entertainment of distinguished state visitors; people who sail together usually establish a quick rapport. At the Cape the *Honey Fitz* gave Kennedy a place to relax or to work in an easy atmosphere. "You don't know what that boat means to me," Kennedy told his naval aide, Captain (now Rear Admiral) Tazewell Shepard, Jr., in 1963.

President Kennedy's affectionate feeling for the Cape was evidenced in the deep interest he took in a project that was dear to his heart: the creation of the Cape Cod National Park, which has preserved that immense, unspoiled outer sweep of beach, sky and ocean for future generations.

His love of the sea, his Cape Cod background and his knowledge of whaling lore, so indigenous to the Cape and the islands, would begin to explain, in part, his interest in scrimshaw.

A lookout atop the foremast scans the horizon for spouting whales. Whaleboats hang in their davits on the port side, ready for lowering. This bark-rigged Yankee whaler proceeds with all sails set on her endless quest for whales. Mounted on a silver base, the scrimshawed tooth is pictured in front of a large model of the Danmark. After the President's death Mrs. Kennedy gave this whale's tooth to General Maxwell Taylor.

History Etched on Ivory　　　　4

For many years past the whaleship has been the pioneer in fer-reting out the remotest and least known parts of the earth. She has explored seas and archipelagos which had no chart, where no Cook or Vancouver had ever sailed.

— HERMAN MELVILLE, *Moby Dick*

THROUGHOUT his life, the subject of history fascinated John F. Kennedy. Histories and biographies of men who made history were his favorite reading material. Heroic men of history furnished examples of right action. Such actions were to be studied and emulated. Public men who ignored history were doomed to repeat the mistakes of the past.

After the President's death, Mrs. Kennedy spoke touchingly of his absorbing interest in history in a conversation with Theodore White:

> I realized history made Jack what he was. You must think of him as this little boy, sick so much of the time, reading in bed, reading history, reading the *Knights of the Round Table,* reading Marlborough. For Jack, history was full of heroes. And if it made him this way — if it made him see the heroes — maybe other little boys will see. Men are such a combination of good and bad. Jack had this hero idea of history, the idealistic view. [1]

A childhood visit to the ancient U.S. frigate *Constitution,* still to this day in active commission at the Charlestown Navy Yard, awakened John Kennedy's earliest interest in history and in all things nautical. Kennedy always maintained a special interest in "Old Ironsides." His grandfather, John F. Fitzgerald, as a member of Congress in 1897, had been instrumental in saving this first ship built for the U.S. Navy as she lay rotting at her dock.

"The sight of that historic frigate with its tall spars and black guns stirred my imagination and made history come alive for me,"[2] Kennedy wrote in recalling his boyhood visits with his grandfather to the *Constitution.* Years later, when he became President, a model of the *Constitution* graced his office in the White House; and he procured yet another model of "Old Ironsides" which he presented to Premier Khrushchev when they conferred in Vienna.

The *Constitution* was designed and constructed by Col. George L. Claghorn, a native of Chilmark, on Martha's Vineyard. Claghorn also turned his hand to the designing and building of whaleships. One of his ships, *Rebecca,* was built in New Bedford, and she was the first of the New Bedford fleet to round Cape Horn in 1792, shortly after news of the multitudes of sperm whales in the Pacific Ocean reached the whaling centers.

The *Rebecca* and the countless whalers that followed her into the Pacific contributed greatly in establishing the young United States as a maritime power. As President, Kennedy stressed again and again the prime importance of maintaining that position of power. Islands which later became American bastions in the far Pacific were discovered and charted by whaling captains. American claims to sovereignty were based on their discoveries as recorded and dated in whaling logbooks and charts. Some of these old whaling maps even played a part in World War II in the South Pacific.

After Pearl Harbor, with war breaking out all over the great Pacific, the Navy found itself with very incomplete geodetic survey information on the tens of thousands of islands and reefs that dotted that immense theater of naval warfare. Hasty studies were made of century-old charts prepared by the whalemen on their roving voyages of exploration in search of new whaling grounds. The old whaling charts proved to be of substantial value in developing new Navy charts for use in the Pacific. It may well be that the charts of the Solomon Islands used by PT 109 Skipper John F. Kennedy were developed from maps originally plotted by the old-time whaling captains.

President Kennedy's interest in scrimshaw was actually whetted by his knowledgeable interest in our maritime history and the pioneering contributions made by the whalemen to that history. It was a Nantucket whaling captain, Timothy Folger, who first plotted the course of that strange ocean river, the Gulf Stream, for his cousin, Benjamin Franklin; in 1820, Captain Nathaniel Palmer, of Stonington, Connecticut, was first to sight Antarctica, the vast continent seven hundred miles south of Cape Horn; it was the whaleman, or rather it was the whale, who first proved the existence of the long-sought Northwest Passage around the top of the world. Whales were taken in the Arctic Ocean north of Alaska in which were found harpoon irons bearing names of ships known to be whaling in Baffin Bay. Whales knew the way through the Northwest Passage if explorers did not.

In 1808 a Nantucket captain, Mayhew Folger, in the *Topaz,* came across the hideaway of the *Bounty* mutineers on lonely Pitcairn Island. Since 1789 the world had wondered what became of Fletcher Christian and his fellow-mutineers.

Whaling captains visited the magnificent harbor at Honolulu in 1818, and from that time the Sandwich Islands, discovered by Captain Cook, became a rendezvous for their whaleships. Magic names and magic places — the Indian Ocean, Madagascar, St. Helena, the Marquesas, Japan, the Sea of Okhotsk, Easter Island with its mysterious stone images, New Zealand — these were as familiar to the whalemen as the streets of their home towns.

In developing the prosperous, if hazardous, whaling industry, they carried the Stars and Stripes all over the globe; they established communications with strange and distant lands, and they helped make America a power on the seas.

On one of the marble-top consoles in the President's office, displayed in front of a large model of the Danmark, Kennedy had a model of a Yankee whaleboat, the clean, swift work boat used in going on and attacking the whale. The model itself is an adequate, modern-day copy of the old whaleboat but not to be compared with a scrimshawed bone model, of which the whalemen made a number. A bone model whaleboat, of course, is about as desirable a piece of skrimshandering as a collector would wish to possess.

There has never been a more seaworthy craft. In open whaleboats, Captain Pollard and Mate Owen Chase with the survivors of the whale-sunk Essex, in 1820 voyaged thirty-seven hundred miles across the Pacific before their eventual rescue off the coast of South America.

The model whaleboat in the Kennedy collection represents the cleanest design, the greatest versatility and seaworthiness of any craft ever built.

The history of whaling, like all history, is the biography of heroes, a subject of profound interest to President Kennedy. Their voyages of discovery and exploration in the endless search for whales carried them into faraway uncharted seas. Their accomplishments as the first American oceanographers loom up like a distant island in the American story. The story of whaling is filled, too, with episodes involving men who faced mutinies, fire at sea, shipwrecks on cannibal coasts and survivors who sailed literally thousands of miles in little open whaleboats.

If President Kennedy was interested in whaling history, the kind of men who created the particular whaling scrimshaw he fancied also engaged his attention. The old-time whalemen were a patriotic lot. They served with distinction in the Revolution and in the War of 1812, when the country was young and facing a cloudy future. Their seamanship and their obvious superiority as boatmen made them most valuable in staffing and manning the ships of the early Navy. Later, whalemen officered and crewed many Navy ships during the Civil War. Whaleships, too, played a part in the Civil War: a sad part, however, as the story of the "Stone Fleet" will reveal a little later.

The whalemen's patriotic sentiments are reflected in the many whales' teeth they scrimshawed with pictures of heroes of the early Republic, ships of the tiny new Navy, patriotic symbols and famous landmarks of liberty. And this was the special kind of scrimshaw that President Kennedy looked for in forming his collection. Here are a few examples:

53

Alexander Hamilton Tooth

The smallish whale's tooth with a rather stern portrait of Alexander Hamilton was one of several displayed in the bookshelves to the left of the President's desk. The back of the tooth is unfinished, showing the rough, ribbed surface of the tooth just as it came from the sperm whale's jawbone.

Kennedy liked to point out that Hamilton, in addition to his other accomplishments, was the father of the Coast Guard, the oldest continuous seagoing service in the United States.

On August 15, 1962, at a review of Coast Guard cadets on the training barque *Eagle*, a beautiful three-masted square-rigger, President Kennedy watched the cadets man the yardarms as it was done in the old days of sail. It was a thrilling sight, and Kennedy complimented the cadets on their performance in words that echoed again his own love of the sea and his respect and admiration for men who follow the sea:

> As a sailor on one of the ships of the Coast Guard this weekend, I realized how important and significant this operation which you've carried out today is. I'm not sure there are many other Americans who could climb that rigging and unfurl those sails in good times and in bad times.

Kennedy went on to recall the part played by Alexander Hamilton as the father of this very ancient service in the country's history, and perhaps there was something more than casual in his reference to the commissioning of the first Coast Guard vessel, *Massachusetts,* at a total cost, fully equipped, of one thousand dollars. A number of members of the Congress and the Secretary of the Treasury, Henry Fowler, had accompanied the President to the review. Mr. Kennedy concluded his remarks to the cadets on the training barque *Eagle* by recalling the high standards set so long ago for the service:

> The mission of the Coast Guard in your manual is to graduate young men with sound bodies, stout hearts and alert minds, with a liking for the sea and its lore, and with that high sense of honor, loyalty and obedience which goes with trained initiative and leadership, well grounded in seamanship, the sciences, and the amenities, and strong in the resolve to be worthy of the traditions of the commissioned officers in the United States Coast Guard, in the service of their country and humanity . . . The words I like best in this very important mission are 'to graduate men with a liking for the sea,' and I know that all of you share the great affection we have for that ever-changing ocean upon which we so much depend. [3]

Three Presidents Tusk

In October 1963, Mrs. John Kennedy bought the scrimshawed walrus tusk bearing portraits of three Presidents. It was to have been a Christmas present for the President, but it was a gift he did not live to open and enjoy.

Between the little seated figure of Justice at the top and the lady with the shield at the base are the portraits of George Washington, the Founding Father, Abraham Lincoln, Preserver of the Union, and Ulysses S. Grant, Lincoln's general in the Civil War and eighteenth President of the United States. But the end of that Civil War also marked the end of the Golden Age of Whaling.

If the Revolutionary War and the War of 1812 had been bad for the business of whaling, the Civil War was disastrous. Confederate privateers ranged the oceans, burning the whaleships at sea. Ships that got back to port safely were not sent out again, because the insurance companies refused to cover them.

Many of the old whaleships served in the war, however, in that strange operation involving the "Stone Fleet." In October 1861, the Navy Department bought a number of ships from the owners in the ports of New Bedford, New London, Mystic, Sag Harbor, Nantucket and Edgartown. The ships, loaded down with stone, were to be sunk at the harbor entrances of the Confederate ports of Charleston and Savannah in an effort to blockade those Southern harbors.

Old New England stone walls furnished the ballast for the ships of the Stone Fleet. Holes were cut in the hulls of the ships and plugs were inserted which could be pulled out to admit the sea when the ships reached their final designated resting place.

On Thanksgiving Day, November 20, 1861, the Stone Fleet, comprising twenty-five ships, sailed from New Bedford, commanded by whaling captains. The crowds on shore waved and cheered, signal guns saluted as the sturdy old whaleships paraded past Clark's Point and out to sea. But the ships were on their way to the graveyard, and the departure on Thanksgiving Day signaled the end of the Golden Age of Whaling.

The Stone Fleet was scuttled in the harbor at Charleston on December 20, 1861. In January 1862, an additional fourteen ships were sunk. The whole operation proved to be useless. Forty-four whaleships in all sank deep in the mud and silt, but vessels of the Confederacy continued to sail in and out of Charleston.

Operation "Stone Fleet" was only one of the disasters of war that overtook the whaling industry. The Confederate cruiser *Alabama*, built and fitted out in England, set out to prey on Northern shipping. Before the *Alabama* was sunk off the coast of France by the U.S.S. *Kearsarge,* she had accounted for seventy Union vessels, fourteen of which were whaleships.

The *Alabama's* first victim was the whaleship *Ocmulgee,* of Edgartown on Martha's Vineyard. By an odd quirk of fate, Raphael Semmes, the Confederate commander of the *Alabama* and Captain Abraham Osborn of the *Ocmulgee* had known each other under happier circumstances before the war.

From 1859 to 1861 Raphael Semmes of the U.S. Navy had served as Secretary of the Lighthouse Board. His work entailed buying whale oil for the lighthouses and this assignment took him to Edgartown. There he was entertained a number of times in the home of whaleship owner Abraham Osborn. Osborn's Wharf, where his ships docked

so long ago, is now occupied by the Edgartown Yacht Club, in whose regattas young John Kennedy often raced.

When the Civil War came, Semmes, born in Maryland, joined the Southern cause. He was given command of the *Alabama*. So it was that the paths of onetime friends crossed again when the *Ocmulgee* was taken by the *Alabama* while cutting in a whale off the Azores. When he recognized his captor, Captain Osborn recalled to Captain Semmes the Osborn family's earlier hospitality in no uncertain terms. But war was war, protests were of no avail, and the oil-laden *Ocmulgee* made a spectacular blaze.

Later that day, Semmes took the *Alabama* close to Flores in the Azores and put off Captain Osborn and his men in their own whaleboats.

Perhaps the worst blow to the whaling fleet came in 1865 after the war was over. The Confederate cruiser *Shenandoah*, unaware, it was claimed, of the end of hostilities, destroyed twenty-nine whaleships in the Arctic fleet. Twenty-four of the ships were burned in six days when the *Shenandoah* came down like a wolf on the fleet in Bering Strait.

The Civil War ended, but the whaling business never really recovered, although the long, slow sunset of whaling lasted another sixty years into the twentieth century.

Bunker Hill Tooth

Bunker Hill Monument really stands on Breed's Hill in Charlestown, Massachusetts, a part of the congressional district John F. Kennedy served for three terms in the House of Representatives in Washington.

The scrimshawed whale's tooth shows the monument after it was completed in 1843. A horsecar with its entrance door in the back between the rear wheels creaks past the great obelisk, and two riders on horseback enter the right foreground.

The cornerstone of the monument was laid on June 17, 1825, on the fiftieth anniversary of the battle. General Lafayette, on his triumphal tour as a guest of the nation, agreed to attend and assist in the ceremonies. Daniel Webster delivered the principal oration to an audience of twenty thousand people which included a number of aged veterans who, like Lafayette, had fought in the Revolution, some of them at Bunker Hill. Notable among these was the Reverend Joseph Thaxter, who had been at Concord Bridge on the 19th of April in '75 and later served as chaplain of Prescott's regiment. Parson Thaxter was designated as the official chaplain to offer the prayer at

the laying of the cornerstone. He traveled to Charlestown from the old whaling port of Edgartown, where he had ministered to the whaling families for more than forty years. Charles E. Banks, in his *History of Martha's Vineyard,* writes that he wore to the end of his life the cocked hat, short clothes, knee and shoe buckles and carried the long cane familiar to the generation that lived during the Revolution. His venerable appearance on that occasion attracted general attention. Thaxter's prayer was quoted in all the papers of the day, and the old chaplain of Prescott's regiment, then past eighty years, was one of the marked figures on that memorable occasion. Fifty years had elapsed since the battle but the sense of nearness and reality had not faded.

The monument was completed in 1843 and Webster delivered a second address to mark the event.

The other side of the Bunker Hill whale's tooth shows an exotic bird of paradise in a border of tropical flowers and foliage. There would not appear to be any connection between the two pictures, and it might be regarded as simply whimsy on the artist's part.

The Vincennes Tusk

The walrus tusk scrimshawed by a sailor on the United States ship *Vincennes* is one of those rare pieces signed and dated by the artist. It is also unusual for being done on a warship rather than a whaler. On the particular voyage when this tusk was scrimshawed there was ample leisure time for carving the tusk.

At the top of the tusk there is etched a double cartouche with the inscription:

Obtained at Gasanup U.S.S. *Vincennes* Aug. 5th. 1855 — H. Johnson U.S. Ship Vincennes.

In March 1855, the *Vincennes,* commanded by Lieutenant John Rodgers, sailed from Hong Kong with orders to survey the islands between Luchu and Japan, then to proceed along the Kurile Islands to Petropaulovski on the Kamchatka Peninsula, and thence north to Bering Strait, the gateway to the Arctic Ocean. At this point Lieutenant Rodgers left a party of men under Lieutenant John M. Brooke. The *Vincennes* cruised north into the Arctic to latitude 72° 5′ N. and longitude 174° 37′ W., sailing over what had been given as land on the admiralty charts. Thence he proceeded to Wrangell Land, but the *Vincennes* was stopped by the ice barrier ten miles from Wrangell. The *Vincennes* had penetrated the north farther than any other American or European ship.

In the meantime our scrimshaw artist, presumably left with Lieutenant Brooke at Bering Strait, obtained the tusk at Gasanup, perhaps in exchange with an Eskimo for tobacco or some other bit of barter, as was the custom.

The *Vincennes* picked up Brooke's party and returned to San Francisco in October 1855. From San Francisco the *Vincennes* sailed around the Horn and arrived back in New York in 1856. This lengthy passage allowed ample time to cover the walrus tusk with the patriotic symbols that decorate this piece. It is a fine memento of one of the *Vincennes's* many notable voyages.

The U.S.S. *Vincennes* was built in the Brooklyn Navy Yard in 1825. She was rated with 18 guns but usually carried 20, was of 700 tons displacement, and had a crew of 190 officers and men. She was called a sloop of war, not as large as a frigate though rigged like one. She would be comparable to a light cruiser in today's Navy.

A great many of her service years were spent in the Pacific, the Antarctic, and the Arctic. In addition to her notable voyages of discovery and exploration, her mission was to protect American merchantmen and whaleships. On one of her rescue missions she brought back survivors of the whaleship *Mentor* who had been held captive by savages when the ship was wrecked in the Pellew Islands.

The *Vincennes* was kept in sound shape all through her years. She circumnavigated the globe three times in a long career. Her final assignment was during the Civil War when she was part of Admiral Farragut's fleet that blockaded the Mississippi River. After the war she was sold at Boston in 1867 for eighty-six hundred dollars.

The old *Vincennes* was a lucky ship, and no other vessel except the *Constitution* served so well on so many missions or sailed as many miles as the doughty little sloop of war *Vincennes*.

Two British Cutters

It would be interesting to know what the sailor had in mind when he scrimshawed this whale's tooth. On one side two British cutters of perhaps eighteen guns each sail close-hauled on a starboard tack, and on the other side an American frigate of twenty guns or more, perhaps the *John Adams,* proceeds serenely on her way. What a surprise lies in store if the cutters and the frigate ever round that headland at the top of the tooth! The meticulous craftsmanship, the knowledgeable execution of the sails and rigging, and the sparing use of color make this a highly desirable piece of scrimshaw. This was one of the pieces that President Kennedy kept on his desk.

COMMODORE
STEPHEN DECATUR, U.S.N.

John Adams

QUINCY, MASS

Decatur-Adams Tusk

The largest of the three walrus tusks in Kennedy's collection is of interest, because it is an unfinished piece of skrimshandering. It shows the preliminary outlining of the subject matter before the artist put in the shading or solid areas to give the pictures form and contrast. It might be compared to the first-state proofing of a copperplate etching.

Above the portrait of Commodore Decatur, King Neptune rides the waves on a fantastic sea horse. Two of his attendant mermen are seen in the water, each blowing a conch shell horn.

Decatur's likeness, a combination of line and stipple dots probably done with a sail needle, is copied from a painting by John Wesley Jarvis.

The head of John Adams, the second President, is taken from a Gilbert Stuart portrait. On the shield below, decorated with stars and stripes that were never completed, is a picture of the old Adams mansion in Quincy, Massachusetts. Two Presidents lived there: John Adams and his son, John Quincy Adams, whose profile in courage was depicted by John F. Kennedy in his Pulitzer Prize-winning book.

The back of the Decatur-Adams tusk is topped by the figure of Justice, probably taken from a woodcut printing ornament of the nineteenth century, as is the vase with flowers. Below the vase a lady poses in a very décolleté ballgown which reveals the swanlike neck and the slope of the shoulders that mark a real beauty. The costume and headdress are of the period of the 1860's. The main illustration on the back, "Love among the roses," shows a gracefully drawn girl holding a basket of roses on her head, little suspecting that Cupid is

The Light of the Lighthouse.

Love among the Roses.

about to unleash his dart. This lovely creature may have been taken from *Godey's Lady's Book,* the fashionable periodical. *Godey's* supplied countless whalemen with pictures of elegantly dressed women, which they copied in their scrimshaw work.

The expertise shown in the lettering and draftsmanship of this tusk would indicate an art skill and ability beyond the talent of the average whaleman. It might be concluded that it was the work of a trained artist or engraver who may have done it at sea or who may have obtained the big tusk from a returning sailor in order to try his hand at scrimshaw.

Free Trade and Sailors' Rights

"Free Trade and Sailors' Rights" was the seamen's motto at the time of the War of 1812,[4] a war that almost brought ruin to the whaling business. Virtually the entire fleet of Nantucket and New Bedford ships was at sea when war was declared. A few of them managed to slip home through the British blockade, but many were captured. Some whaleships were taken into British ports, but most were burned at sea. According to Edouard Stackpole, a reward of five hundred dollars was offered to any Martha's Vineyard pilot who would bring a whaleship safely into Old Town Harbor, as Edgartown was then known.

In the War of 1812, President Madison had a Navy comprising twenty-four vessels in all. During the war, thirteen of these were lost. When John F. Kennedy became President, the United States had become the greatest sea power on earth. In Kennedy's speeches, he emphasized again and again the importance of maintaining that sea power. (Just how important it was became apparent in the Cuban missile crisis when his blockade of Cuba was a most effective factor in reaching a settlement with the Russians.)

When the President and Mrs. Kennedy lived in the White House, the only article in the old mansion that dated back to its first occupancy by John and Abigail Adams in 1800 was the great, full-length portrait of George Washington by Gilbert Stuart, which narrowly escaped destruction in the War of 1812.

The city of Washington was taken, and the White House was burned by the British in 1814, in retaliation, they said, for the destruction of the capital buildings at Toronto by the Americans in 1813. As the British approached, Dolly Madison refused to quit the President's House until the picture of Washington could be secured. The frame itself was screwed to the wall, so it was broken up, and Mrs. Madison escaped with the canvas. The portrait now hangs in the elegant white and gold East Room, where the President and Mrs. Kennedy entertained with the graceful style that was a hallmark of his Administration.

Decatur Tooth

Like the folk art paintings of the nineteenth century, very few pieces of scrimshaw were signed by the artist-sailors, and many of their portrait subjects, ships and whaling scenes are not identified by helpful titling.

This handsomely executed whale's tooth, even though the top is chipped, is a real prize with a notable historic connection. The officer wears the dashing, high-collared Navy uniform of the period of 1812, and American flags frame the portrait. On the back of the tooth there is an urn with flowers, and so we may assume this scrimshaw to be a memorial tribute. This clue narrows down the search for the identity of the portrait's subject. The officer is Commodore Stephen Decatur, and the portrait is taken from a painting by Gilbert Stuart. The whale-man who scrimshawed Decatur's likeness copied it from an engraving by David Edwin of Stuart's painting, and the urn of flowers would indicate it was done some time after Decatur's death in 1820.

74

There is an unusual link between the Decatur tooth and the whale's tooth with the portrait of William Henry Allen in the Kennedy collection. Decatur was the friend and mentor of Captain Allen, who had served with distinction under Decatur in the capture of the *Macedonian* by the *United States*. In 1820 Decatur was killed in a duel with the luckless, tarnished Commodore James Barron. It will be recalled that Barron, commanding the *Chesapeake*, was not prepared to fight when he was fired on and surrendered to H.M.S. *Leopard* in 1807. Young William Henry Allen, then a third lieutenant on the *Chesapeake*, had fired the single cannon shot that returned the *Leopard's* sudden, point-blank broadside.

Stephen Decatur served in the old Navy in the days of the tough sea dog, when officers were expected to be of "stout hearts and alert minds, with a liking for the sea and its lore, and with that high sense of honor, loyalty and obedience which goes with trained initiative and leadership," as President Kennedy remarked to the cadets of the Coast Guard training barque *Eagle* in August 1962.

Decatur was born in 1779 and joined the Navy as a midshipman in 1798, gaining initial fame for his exploits in command of the brig *Enterprise* against the Tripoli corsairs in 1803. He was promoted to captain in 1804, and his subsequent career showed him to be as courageous an officer as the Navy ever had.

Nowadays, the commanding officer of a Navy vessel is in constant communication with his GHQ for instructions in case of crisis, and a long chain of command can cause fatal complications. In Decatur's day, the commanding officer was on his own, only knowing that it was

his duty to defend the country's interest at all times, in all places, and at all costs. Decatur's simple creed was summed up in a toast which he offered at a state banquet:

Our country! In her intercourse with foreign nations may she always be in the right; but our country, right or wrong![5]

The circumstances which prompted Decatur's famous words were not unlike those that exist in the 1960's. The War of 1812 was a very unpopular war with people who lived along the Eastern seaboard. In New England, whose ox was indeed gored, there was open talk of state's rights and threats of secession. Jefferson and Madison were both vilified: Jefferson for having set the stage for war with the Embargo Act and Madison for declaring an actual state of war with England. The opposition to an unpopular war by many Federalist newspapers and their supporters of that day does not differ greatly from the resistance that recent administrations have met in their conduct of what they considered to be the national policy. The end of the War of 1812 was not an unqualified victory for the United States. In the Treaty of Ghent, England did not foreswear her declared right to impress sailors or seize ships, but such things did not happen again.

Decatur's famed statement was made after the war had ended. It expressed his own feelings in answer to those who had objected to the war and not supported the government. It was the loyal credo of a Navy man who had served his country well. It was not regarded as "chauvinistic" by Americans of that day. Bruce Catton, the famed historian, noted that generations of schoolchildren memorized Decatur's words, and adult Americans kept the slogan handy as a good rule of thumb for a national crisis.

The two sides of this whale's tooth carried an important message for Americans at the time it was scrimshawed by some unknown whaleman. On one side of the tooth twenty stars indicate the American flag adopted in 1818. The lady with the flag and anchor is garbed in the costume of that period. Perhaps she represents Commerce, or Free Trade, or Prosperity, since she doesn't wear the traditional accouterments associated with the figure of Liberty. In the background a shipowner's house flag flies at the masthead.

The men who fought for and defended the early Republic have become, more and more, legendary symbols, images from the long ago and faraway past, misty and half-forgotten in this modern day. But to the old whalers, these notable men and their deeds were real and admirable. They were honored by the whalemen, and the sailors' tribute was inscribed on the polished ivory whales' teeth and walrus tusks which John F. Kennedy collected.

The other side of the tooth shows a Navy frigate sailing the ocean with her guns prepared and ready for action.

In the early nineteenth century American commercial shipping interests and the whaling industry were frequently forced to call on the government for protection as they went about their business on the oceans of the world. A number of whaleships were seized and looted by piratical Spanish governors on the west coast of South America. The message etched on this whale's tooth would seem to be that a strong Navy was needed if the nation's business was to compete successfully on the seas. Nearly a century and a half later, President Kennedy stated on numerous occasions the continuing need to maintain an American Navy second to none.

Scrimshawed Symbols of Courage 5

. . . if a man made up his mind to live, mere sickness could not kill him; nothing but a whale, or a gale, or some violent, ungovernable, unintelligent destroyer of that sort.

— HERMAN MELVILLE, *Moby Dick*

John Kennedy regarded courage as "that most admirable of human virtues." It is a quality that was of first importance in the dangerous business of whaling.

The whalemen were a tough and courageous breed whose valor was recognized nearly two centuries ago by Thomas Jefferson in his Whale Memorial to the French Minister in 1778: "The Spermacetti Whale found by the Nantuckois, is an active, fierce animal, and requires vast address and boldness in the fisherman."[1]

In the little speeches they made to the crews at the beginning of each whaling voyage, the captains asked, "What are you here for?" Older hands knew the answer and greenhorns learned fast. The business was to kill whales, get oil, and the sooner the casks were filled, the sooner they could sail home. "A dead whale or a stove boat" was the whaling motto, and the words were engraved in the sea hunter's mind as they were on hundreds of whales' teeth. In the business of whaling, success depended on the spirit brought to the job. Every officer and every harpooneer first had to prove his courage beyond any shadow of a doubt. But fighting a sperm whale took more than just skill and courage. Clifford Ashley, who made a whaling voyage long ago in the old bark *Sunbeam,* stated that "Success depended largely upon sheer ferocity of attack, of total submergence of all thought except that of getting into an advantageous position at the earliest moment and getting fast ahead of any other boat. It was the spirit of competition between boats . . . 'whaling for glory,' it was called.[2]" In essence, sheer ferocity of attack in whaling is not unlike the political maneuver of "going for the jugular."

Some knowledge of the savage nature and habits of the sperm

whale, whose teeth and bone furnished the lovely material for scrimshaw, should help us to realize the raw courage it took to harpoon, lance and kill the fiercest animal that ever lived.

The sperm whale lives on giant squid, which he finds in the fathomless black depths. Some authorities say that there are more squid on the ocean bed than any other living creatures on earth. They must have existed in great numbers to have supplied the sperm whale's bill of fare for so many aeons. Now that the sperm whale stock is so depleted, perhaps there is a hideous imbalance of writhing masses of immense squid on the ocean floor. The sperm whale chewed up squid in great gobbets, swallowing the sharp cuttlefish bones which often lodged in his alimentary canal. Around these distress points, ambergris formed. When whalemen took a particularly thin and scrawny sperm whale, his carcass was carefully checked for ambergris, which was a most valuable ingredient in the making of perfumes. To the whale it may have been like having an ulcer, adding to his already cantankerous nature.

Sperm whales migrated from one whaling ground to another as regularly as clockwork. They traveled, said Melville, in "veins" of the ocean, never varying from these paths. Whether they followed migrating squid is not known to this day. It may be that, like certain other animals, they moved on to other fields, always leaving enough squid to replenish the feeding grounds for their next hungry visit.

Sperm whales, unlike other whales, traveled in schools or "pods." Other whales are monogamous, but one bull sperm served a number of cow whales. Whalemen called the biggest bull whale the schoolmaster.

A bull sperm whale is a terrible and cunning fighter, "fights at both ends," the whalemen said. His long jawbone full of huge teeth could chew a whaleboat to kindling wood in a trice. He fought, too, with his flukes; when he thrashed, or "lobtailed" the ocean surface with these giant flukes, it is said that the noise could be heard several miles away. The sperm whale's immense mallet-shaped head was, in itself, a dreadful weapon with which he rammed and bashed in whaleboats and even sank entire whaleships in his fury. The sinking by an enraged sperm whale of the whaleship *Essex* in 1820 is the most well-known disaster, but there were a number of other vessels sunk by angry whales. When a sperm whale was approached, he often "pitch-poled," raising his huge head high out of the water, bobbing up and down in a circle as his little eyes took in the entire scene and located his tormentors. When a sperm whale pitch-poled, it was regarded as a very unfriendly sign by the whalemen.

One of President Kennedy's scrimshaw items, most interesting for its connection with a daring bit of whaling history, is the old tooth etched with a picture of the ship *Hector*, studding sails set, approaching bow-on. The story is taken from the log of the *Hector* in the Old Dartmouth Historical Society Whaling Museum and from Starbuck's *History of Nantucket*. It is well told by Edouard Stackpole in *The Sea-Hunters:*

Captain John O. Morse in the *Hector*, of New Bedford (October, 1832), commanded a crew of twenty-seven men, the oldest being thirty-two years, only five men over twenty-five years of age, and twelve men of nineteen years. This was practically an all-Martha's Vineyard crew, and two of the officers, Thomas Norton and George Luce, later became famous whalemen.

Some years after, the mate, Thomas Norton, then a shipmaster, told of the attack made by a bull sperm whale on several of the *Hector's* boats. In describing the incident, he stated that the whale himself took the initiative, while the boats were approaching him. Mate Norton's boat was first "on," but the moment the harpoon struck, the bull sperm, with one flick of his flukes, stove in the boat's bow. By drawing the sail under the bow, the boat was kept free of water, and Mate Norton resumed the attack.

In the meantime, Captain Morse came up in his boat and was warned off by Mate Norton. But the ship's master had a long lance which he thought would do the trick and proceeded to the attack. The sperm was an extraordinary antagonist. Slipping over on his back, he caught the Captain's boat in his mouth and literally shook it to pieces.

Mate Norton's and Second Officer Luce's boats picked up Captain Morse and his men. Norton was anxious to return to the attack. With a picked crew in the remaining undamaged boat, he approached the fighting whale.

Then followed a battle royal: the frail boat carefully advancing, then retreating at 'starn all for your lives!' The infuriated whale surging forward, driving to attack from under the surface of the sea, flashing his terrible jaw at the nimbly-handled boat, beating the sea with tremendous blows of his deadly flukes. In a radius of half a mile the fight continued — until, seizing the opening he had been awaiting, Mate Norton had his boat "wood to blackskin" and with swift probings of his lance, brought a sudden end to the battle. Here was a triumph of skilled whalemen. [3]

The log of the *Hector* records that the whale made sixty barrels of oil. Two toggle irons from the Nantucket whaleship *Barclay* were found imbedded in the whale. Two months previously the mate of the *Barclay* had been killed when the whale smashed his boat.

What a trophy of the hunt it would be if the *Hector* tooth in President Kennedy's collection came from the bull sperm whale Mate Norton took so long ago.

On the other side of the *Hector* tooth, the ship *Charles* floats by under full sail. The shysail, rarely used on whalers, indicates that the ship may be making a passage to new whaling grounds, or perhaps she is a full ship, homeward bound. It would be reasonable to assume that the sailor who scrimshawed the tooth had made voyages in both ships. It was not uncommon for a whale-hunter to go out in one ship and return years later in another. Both the *Hector* and the *Charles* made some notable voyages, and the stories of their greasy luck make this tooth a highly interesting item in the Kennedy collection.

In the 1820's the ship *Charles*, of New Bedford, commanded by Captain Joy, made a remarkably successful voyage to the South Atlantic, bringing back two thousand barrels of oil after being out only seven months and twenty days, sailing to the coast of Patagonia. Filling the ship in such short time, there must have been very little leisure for scrimshawing on that particular cruise of the *Charles*.

The New Hebrides and the Solomon Islands, the theater of Lieutenant John Kennedy's war in the South Pacific, were frequented by Yankee whaleships long ago. In the listing of Pacific Ocean whaling grounds, we find that sperm whales were once abundant around the Solomon Islands, and humpback whales were taken in the waters around the New Hebrides.

His years of sailing and his familiarity with boats and the water helped John Kennedy when he applied for a commission in the Navy at the advent of World War II. Assignment to PT boats, those fast, powerful little seahunters was just the kind of duty that appealed to young Jack Kennedy.

Captain Tazewell Shepard, Jr., Kennedy's naval aide when he became President, wrote that "Jack Kennedy had all the qualifications: he was an athlete and a good swimmer, he had extensive experience in handling small craft, and he was intelligent."[4]

Where whalemen of an earlier day sought to engage sperm whales in savage combat, the PT 109 skipper patrolled the same shark-infested waters, hunting for Japanese destroyers.

The story of the sinking of Kennedy's PT 109 in Blackett Strait on an August night in 1943 and the courage, endurance and leadership he showed before he and his crew were rescued are too well known to need repeating here. Lieutenant Kennedy won the Navy and Marine Corps Medal, as well as the Purple Heart for injuries received on the night his boat was stove, but one of the souvenirs of his war service that Kennedy prized most highly was a piece of coconut shell from Nauru, one of the small islands in the vicinity of the PT 109 disaster.

(The whalemen in the South Seas often used coconut shells in their scrimshaw work, principally in the making of dippers. The polished coconut shells formed natural dippers, and the handles were made of exotic woods and pieces of whale ivory, sometimes handsomely inlaid with mother-of-pearl.)

The piece of coconut shell that Kennedy treasured had a message scratched on it by a shipwrecked sailor, and it might be described as a sort of scrimshawing done under great pressure.

It is, of course, the famous coconut shell on which Lieutenant John Kennedy carved a message after his PT 109 was sliced in half by the Japanese destroyer. He gave the message on the piece of shell to a native, telling him to deliver it to the PT base at Rendova:

NAURU ISL NATIVE KNOWS POSIT
AND REEFS 11 ALIVE NEED
SMALL BOAT KENNEDY

Long after the war was over, the piece of coconut shell on which the castaway skipper had "scrimshawed" his call for help came back to him. Mounted and encased in plastic, it sat on his desk when he was President. That incident in the Solomon Islands involving the destruction of PT 109 inspired an ex-whaler from Brooklyn, an ardent Kennedy admirer, to create a modern, three-piece scrimshaw ensemble, which he presented to the President.

Etched on the large whale's tooth, a giant sperm whale smashes a whaleboat to kindling as the crewmen leap and swim for their lives. The tooth is inscribed with the old battle cry of whalemen, "A dead whale or a stove boat." Hundreds of light whaleboats were stove by whales in the South Pacific of long ago, many in the very waters in which Skipper Kennedy sought his foe in World War II. The comparison was obvious to the old whaler, who carved a thin slice from a whale's tooth and etched the enemy Japanese destroyer about to ram the PT 109 to her doom, even as Moby Dick, the great white whale, stove in the ancient *Pequod*. The third piece of ivory on the wooden base is intended to simulate the Nauru Island coconut shell on which Kennedy scratched his call for help.

As Croswell Bowen pointed out, in an article in *American Heritage:* "Both the harpooner and the PT boat skipper risked sudden and violent death as they stalked their quarry. Both fulfilled the Ernest Hemingway definition of courage — grace under pressure — which Kennedy quoted in his *Profiles in Courage*. During the war, Skipper Kennedy, of course, survived a stove boat with considerable grace." [5]

Kennedy went into the Navy a boy and came out a man "tempered by war," as he described his own generation in his Inaugural Address in 1961. What he saw, what he experienced of war, what he learned helped to mold the core and character of the man; and the public offices which he was to fill benefited in countless ways by his experiences. The Navy, its men and the purposes it serves always had a warm place in Kennedy's heart. The scrimshawed whales' teeth in his collection, etched with pictures of ships of the Old Navy, evidenced that admiration. Typical of these is the William Henry Allen tooth, a present from Mrs. Kennedy.

Allen Street, a fashionable address in the New York City of 1813, was named in his honor, but who today remembers handsome young William Henry Allen, Esq.? He is an all-but-forgotten Navy hero of the War of 1812 who fell, mortally wounded, when the United States brig *Argus,* under his command, engaged H.M.S. *Pelican* in St. George's Channel. The *Argus* had been wreaking havoc on British shipping in the waters between Ireland and England.

Wm Henry Allen

This scrimshawed tooth, done by an unknown sailor with that strong feeling of patriotism so natural to all whalemen, is noteworthy not only for its historic naval connection, but for its technical excellence as a beautiful specimen of scrimshaw work. The portrait and the signature title were faithfully copied by the whaleman from a stippled engraving by David Edwin which served as a frontispiece illustration for an account of Captain Allen's gallant career in *The Portfolio* issue of January 1814. The classic profile portrait of Master Commandant William Henry Allen and the little squadron of warships on the reverse side of the tooth made this scrimshaw item as choice as any in the Kennedy collection. Very few pictures compose as nicely on the rounded white background of a whale's tooth as the etchings on this particular piece of scrimshaw.

William Henry Allen was born in Providence, Rhode Island, on October 21, 1784, the son of General William Allen, who had served with distinction in the Revolutionary War. His mother was the sister of William Jones, the Governor of Rhode Island during the War of 1812. Young Allen entered the Navy as a midshipman in May 1800, six months short of his sixteenth birthday. His early Navy years were served mostly in the Mediterranean, on the frigates *George Washington, Philadelphia, John Adams,* and *Congress,* in which he was appointed sailing master under Captain John Rodgers. In 1805 he sailed with Rodgers in the *Constitution,* where he was made third lieutenant.

In 1807, Lieutenant Allen was assigned to the unlucky ship *Chesapeake* under Commodore Barron, and Allen fired the only shot against H.M.S. *Leopard* in the ignominious affair off Norfolk when the totally unprepared Barron was attacked and struck his colors.

Allen stayed with *Chesapeake* until 1809, when he was assigned to the *United States* as first officer under Commodore Stephen Decatur.

The high point of Allen's Navy career came in October 1812, when the *United States* defeated H.M.S. *Macedonian* in a rousing sea battle. Decatur highly commended Lieutenant Allen in his report of the victory, attributing his superiority in gunnery over the *Macedonian* to Allen's exertions in training the men to the guns. To Allen he assigned the honor of sailing the battered *Macedonian* to New York, where a hero's welcome awaited the prize crew.

Allen was promoted to captain, and in the spring of 1813, Decatur procured for him the command of the United States brig *Argus.* The *Argus* was built in Boston in 1803. She was of 298 tonnage, and she was rated as carrying 16 guns, with a crew of around 120 men.

Captain Allen's first assignment was to take William Henry Crawford to his new post as minister to France. Allen managed to avoid the British warships on patrol in the English Channel, and he sailed the *Argus* to Lorient in Brittany, where he landed his distinguished passenger.

Allen's orders were then to proceed to destroy as much British merchant shipping as he might encounter in the waters around the British Isles. In the following weeks Captain Allen in the *Argus* made raid after raid on English shipping, the destruction amounting to an estimated two million five hundred thousand dollars. In each encounter, passengers and crew were permitted to take their personal belongings before the captured ship was burned, and the English found nothing to object to in Allen's treatment of his prisoners. But the British merchants and insurance companies were in a panic at their losses, and British warships were out in force to catch up with the *Argus*. On August 14, 1813, H.M.S. *Pelican* finally did.

In the dark hours before dawn, the *Argus* was standing by a large British merchantman, which had been taken and set afire after the removal of passengers and crew. The brig *Pelican*, commanded by Captain Maples, saw the flames in the night and headed for her encounter with the *Argus*. The *Pelican* brig, of 385 tonnage, was larger than Captain Allen's *Argus*, but Allen had stated many times that he would not avoid a fight with any two-masted ship. And so in the morning's first light, the battle was joined.

In the first minutes of the engagement Captain Allen's left leg was all but taken off by a cannon shot. He remained on deck, however, until he fainted from loss of blood and was carried below. Allen's first officer took charge until he was hit by grapeshot. The command then passed to the second officer, who continued to fight the ship, but by this time the *Argus* had become unmaneuverable. With her rigging shot away, she lay in the water at the mercy of the *Pelican*. Allen's first officer, his head wrapped in bandages, came back on deck to take charge, but nothing could be done except strike the colors. And so the sea fight ended with the *Pelican's* capture of the *Argus*.

Captain Allen's leg was amputated by the ship's surgeon of the *Argus*, and he was taken in the captured vessel to Plymouth, England, after the ship had been repaired enough to sail. He died in Mill Prison Hospital August 18, 1813, and was buried with full military honors, eight British Navy captains acting as pallbearers. Captain Allen was twenty-eight years old.

Those who have served as Presidents agree that no man ever enters the White House really ready for the responsibilities of the Office, with its myriad unpredictable problems. The Office itself makes the man.

In December 1962, after two years in the White House, President Kennedy said: "There is no experience you can get that can possibly prepare you adequately for the Presidency . . ." [6]

There has never been a man who aspired to the Presidency, however, who didn't do the best he could to train himself for the job; and every President has entered his term with the determination to serve the whole nation and all its people to the best of his ability. But no President can be all things to all people.

"Nine years in Congress," wrote Kennedy in 1955, "have taught me the wisdom of Lincoln's words: 'There are few things wholly evil or wholly good. Almost everything, especially of government policy, is an inseparable compound of the two, so that our best judgement of the preponderance between them is continually demanded.' " [7]

The Lincoln quotation is from *Profiles in Courage,* which Kennedy wrote with the research help of Theodore Sorensen. The book was written while the then-Senator was recovering from his final, successful spine operation in 1955. In the long period of painful hospitalization and slow convalescence, Senator Kennedy began to write the book that won him a Pulitzer Prize in the field of history.

Profiles in Courage is a book about courage and politics, as Kennedy said. It is, moreover, a distillation of John F. Kennedy's own code. What he found admirable in the courageous acts of those public men whose profiles make up the book tells us fully as much about a young author and Senator who was to become the thirty-fifth President

98

of the United States. The book is a blueprint for any man who would serve his country well, yet there is one vital ingredient missing. As Kennedy wrote, "The stories of past courage can define that ingredient — they can teach, they can offer hope, they can provide inspiration — but they cannot supply courage itself. For this each man must look into his own soul." [8]

If stories of courage can define that ingredient, there is also in certain tangible objects that same power to teach, to offer hope, or provide inspiration: such things as President Kennedy chose in the decoration of his White House office. There were the sword and part of the tattered jack of Commodore John Barry, "Father of the American Navy"; ship models that included the *Constitution,* the great clipper *Flying Cloud,* and Kennedy's own PT 109; splendid naval paintings such as the engagement of the *Bonhomme Richard* and the British *Serapis,* the victory of the *Constitution* over *Guerrière* in the War of 1812; the historic desk in the room, made from the timbers of H.M.S. *Resolute,* the ship that was found abandoned in the far north by the New London whaler, *George Henry;* and the numerous scrimshawed whales' teeth that Kennedy collected. Each and every one of those whales' teeth had been taken long ago in ferocious combat with sperm whales.

After the President's death, Robert Kennedy presented this whale's tooth from the collection to LeMoyne Billings, John Kennedy's friend and classmate, who had been so helpful to the President in forming his collection. On the tooth is a big frigate of the old Navy, her sails furled on her cloud-scraping masts, her netting guard set to repel boarders.

Scrimshaw and Creative Expression 6

It seems to me that the philosophers were right who claimed that the value of art lies in its effect and from this drew the corollary that its value lies not in beauty, but in right action. For an effect is idle unless it is effective. If art is no more than pleasure, no matter how spiritual, it is of no great consequence . . . Art, unless it leads to right action, is no more than the opium of an intelligentsia.

— W. Somerset Maugham, *A Writer's Notebook*

SCRIMSHAW is recognized today as original American folk art developed by the whalemen to relieve the seemingly endless monotony, the mind-shattering idleness on their long voyages. The whaleman sought to express himself in carving with his jackknife articles of beauty and usefulness from the enduring sea ivory of the whale. As Clifford Ashley pointed out many years ago, the very beauty of the material gave even the crudest work a certain charm, and the best examples of scrimshaw may be ranked as fine art. In etching a sailing ship on a whale's tooth, the sailor was sure of himself. He knew his subject, and he had no peer in depicting a ship on the ocean. Eighteen of the scrimshawed pieces in Kennedy's collection bore pictures of sailing ships, some of them whalers, others ships of the old Navy.

As we have seen, the whaleman's creative self-expression was also evidenced in whales' teeth etched with the patriotic subjects he admired and honored: historic American scenes, monuments of freedom, heroes of the early Republic and symbols of the whaleman's patriotism — liberty, justice, the American eagle, Old Glory, Columbia with her shield and anchor. Whales' teeth of this sort, scrimshawed with pictures that mirrored the sailor's love of country, were well represented in the President's collection. Symbols inscribed on whales' teeth perhaps gave the President's wife her thoughtful idea for the unique piece of modern scrimshaw she commissioned as a Christmas present for her husband.

In the summer of 1962, the townspeople of Fairhaven, across the Acushnet River from New Bedford, had presented the President with a whale's tooth on which Milton Delano, a local artist and engineer, etched John F. Kennedy's likeness. The portrait tooth was beautifully

executed by one of the few living men who worked in the old, time-consuming, traditional way of scrimshawing. Kennedy was delighted with the gift and expressed his high admiration for Mr. Delano's ability as a scrimshaw artist.

Delano's work on the portrait tooth led to Mrs. Kennedy's request that he scrimshaw the Seal of the President of the United States on a whale's tooth.

Kennedy had described the device on the Presidential Seal to make a point in his Annual Message to Congress on the State of the Union, January 30, 1961. The President listed some of the problems facing his Administration, and, he continued:

To meet this array of challenges — to fulfill the role we cannot avoid on the world scene — we must reexamine and revise our whole arsenal of tools: military, economic and political.

One must not overshadow the other. On the Presidential Coat of Arms, the American eagle holds in his right talon the olive branch, while in his left he holds a bundle of arrows. We intend to give equal attention to both. [1]

Milton Delano obtained an enormous nine-and-a-half-inch bull whale's tooth — from a "genuine old sog," as the whalemen would say — that had been brought to New Bedford in the year 1818. He spent two hundred and forty hours etching, coloring and polishing an ornate, early nineteenth century version of the Seal on the ancient ivory, changing only the number of stars in the border to fifty. The giant tooth was then mounted on a base of walnut taken from the captain's cabin of the old Dartmouth whaling bark *Sunbeam*. On a sparkling October day Delano delivered it to Mrs. Kennedy at the summer White House in Hyannis Port.

The President was absolutely enchanted with his present on Christmas morning in 1962. He treasured it not only as a beautiful work of scrimshaw, but for the thoughtful and loving interest that prompted the gift. From that day, the huge tooth held the place of honor on the right-hand corner of his desk. Understandably, it always meant more to him than any other piece in his scrimshaw collection. This huge tooth, trophy of the sea hunt, taken so long ago in head-on savage combat with leviathan in all his brute energy, and now inscribed with the Seal of the President of the United States, was placed by Mrs. Kennedy in the President's coffin, and it went with him to his grave.

President Kennedy and his First Lady brought youth and a graceful elegance to the White House, with a gracious and easy style that intrigued their fellow Americans and charmed the people of countries abroad. When they entertained, it was with a thoughtfulness and flair that had not been seen at 1600 Pennsylvania Avenue in many years. Together, they shared a deep interest in creative expression and a desire to honor people of the arts. That recognition was noted on the day Kennedy took office, when he invited the aged New England poet, Robert Frost, to read a poem Frost had composed for the occasion. Later, at Amherst College in 1963, Kennedy spoke of the significant place that art should have in our society:

When power leads man toward arrogance, poetry reminds him of his limitations. When power narrows the area of man's concern, poetry reminds

This whale's tooth — etched with pictures of Independence Hall, flowers, grapevines, leafy foliage and portraits quite Daguerrean in feeling — fits admirably with Melville's description of scrimshaw "as closely packed in its maziness of design as the Greek savage, Achilles's shield." Every inch of this large tooth is richly decorated.

The steeple on the old building was removed in 1781 but was restored in 1828. President Kennedy's whale's tooth, showing the restored steeple, was copied by the sailor from a published engraving of that time.

The three portraits on this tooth would appear to have been copied from daguerreotypes, treasured pictures of loved ones which the whaleman probably kept in his sea chest. Might they be his mother and two sisters? Daguerreotypes, invented in 1839, were much in vogue in the 1840's and '50's, and this scrimshawed tooth may be ascribed to that period in Whaling's Golden Age.

him of the richness and diversity of his existence. When power corrupts, poetry cleanses. For art establishes the basic human truth which must serve as the touchstone of our judgement. The artist . . . becomes the last champion of the individual mind and sensibility against an intrusive society and an officious state . . . I see little of more importance to the future of our country and our civilization than full recognition of the place of the artist. If art is to nourish the roots of our culture, society must set the artist free to follow his vision wherever it takes him. We must never forget that art is not a form of propaganda; it is a form of truth. [2]

In the White House, the President and Mrs. Kennedy did a great deal to increase our awareness and knowledge of our cultural heritage. Mrs. Kennedy's talent and taste in decorating did much to refurbish the White House in its arrangements and furnishings, providing a setting that reflected our national culture and our historic past. Her intense interest in the President's House generated others' enthusiasm, and a number of antique pieces acquired by early Presidents were returned to their original home.

The Kennedys, of that new generation born in this fast-changing twentieth century, nevertheless believed in maintaining all the traditional and original dignity of the White House. This was particularly evident in the furnishings of the President's office.

Shortly after moving into the White House, Mrs. Kennedy came across a curiously carved old desk in one of the storage rooms. It bore an inscribed brass plate with an interesting reference to an American whaling captain and his ship:

H.M.S. "RESOLUTE," forming part of the expedition in search of SIR JOHN FRANKLIN in 1852, was abandoned in latitude 74°41′N. longitude 101°22′W. on 15th May 1854. She was discovered and extricated in September 1855, in latitude 67°N. by Captain Buddington of the United States whaler "*George Henry*." The ship was purchased, fitted out and sent to England, as a gift to her Majesty Queen Victoria by the President and People of the United States, as a token of goodwill and friendship. This table was made from timbers when she was broken up, and is presented by the QUEEN of GREAT BRITAIN & IRELAND TO THE PRESIDENT OF THE UNITED STATES, as a memorial of the courtesy and loving kindness which dictated the offer of the gift of the "RESOLUTE."

The "table" was presented to President Rutherford B. Hayes in the late 1870's.

Polished up again and installed in the President's office, the old *Resolute* desk recalled an almost forgotten page in English and American history, dating back to the Administration of President Franklin Pierce.

Sir John Franklin's expedition into the Arctic to discover the Northwest Passage disappeared in 1845. Over the following years, a number of relief expeditions, both English and American, were sent north to search for the lost explorers, and some of these rescue ships, among them H.M.S. *Resolute,* were abandoned and lost in the ice.

The search ship *Resolute* had been abandoned in May 1854, at Melville Island in the vicinity of what was known as the Post Office of the North Pole, and had "drifted down the country" for a distance of twelve hundred miles in a period of fourteen months. In his excellent book, *The Arctic Whalers,* Basil Lubbock recounts the story of the extraordinary recovery of the *Resolute:*

On September 17, 1855, the American whaling barque *George Henry* was working her way past masses of floating ice, near the entrance to Cumberland Straits, when she sighted a ship bearing N.E., about twenty miles from Cape God's Mercy. The stranger's head was pointed due east, and as she never altered this direction it was evident that she was a derelict. For five days the two ships slowly approached each other, then on the sixth, Captain James Buddington, master of the *George Henry* and late mate of the *MacLellan,* lowered his boats and boarded the stranger, which, to his amazement, he found to be the discovery ship *Resolute.* Handing over his own ship to his mate, with orders to take her straight home to New London, Connecticut, he, with part of his crew, gallantly took charge of the derelict. I say "gallantly," because the risks in undertaking this salvage were such as few men would have voluntarily undergone. The *Resolute's* hold was full of water, which it took three days to pump out; nearly everything aboard was destroyed or rotten, with the exception of several casks of salt junk. A large library of Arctic books in the cabin were frozen into blocks of ice and had to be thrown overboard. An immense quantity of clothes were also found frozen stiff. What was more surprising was that a large amount of whalebone was found aboard, and it was concluded that this had been bought from the Eskimos. The derelict's armament, a brass cannon and Minie rifles, was in perfect order, but her sails were so rotten that one could poke one's fingers through them like brown paper.

After a long and perilous voyage with continual headwinds, Captain Buddington succeeded in bringing the *Resolute* safely back to his home port of New London. The American government then performed a very gracious act of courtesy; Congress purchased the *Resolute* from Captain Buddington and his crew for $40,000, refitted her and sent her across to England under a captain of the United States Navy as a present to Queen Victoria. [3]

In President Kennedy's Conference Room in the West Wing there was a fine old engraving over the mantel entitled "England and America." It commemorates the occasion of Queen Victoria's visit to the *Resolute* when it was returned to England by the United States in 1856.

The desk made from the ancient oak timbers of the *Resolute,* its top liberally decorated with scrimshawed whales' teeth, dovetailed nicely with all the other mementoes of the sea in Kennedy's office.

The nautical memorabilia, the paintings of ships and the scrimshawed whales' teeth atop the old *Resolute* desk and around the room added a special flavor and virile character to the general atmosphere of grace and elegance in his office. The room with its furnishings possessed a rare magic which had the power to evoke for the visitor those moments of courage and destiny significant and dear to all Americans.

In the Executive Mansion President Kennedy and his First Lady exercised a genius for communicating a deep and loving sense of the American past in their decorative tastes, and they wished to share all this with the American people. No other house in America, with all its historical associations, evokes greater sentiments of patriotism in the visitor or more dedicated purpose in its occupants.

President Kennedy was very fond of the whale's tooth inscribed with an early view of the President's House. He liked the original designation, the President's House, as the White House was called when John Adams first moved in on November 1, 1800; and when the Kennedys lived there one hundred and sixty years later, he showed his partiality in the little matchboxes used in the family quarters with "The President's House" printed on the covers.

The mansion was designed and built by James Hoban, who won a gold medal in the competition for the assignment in 1792. The scrimshawed etching of the President's House in Kennedy's collection shows the South Front with the oval portico added by Thomas Jefferson's friend, architect Benjamin Latrobe, in 1824, and the picture must have been copied from an engraving of that period.

The night after John Adams moved into the still unfinished President's House he wrote a letter to his wife Abigail in which he penned the lines that President Franklin D. Roosevelt caused to be carved on the mantel in the state dining room:

I pray Heaven to bestow the best of blessings on this House and all that shall hereafter inhabit it. May none but honest and wise men ever rule under this roof.

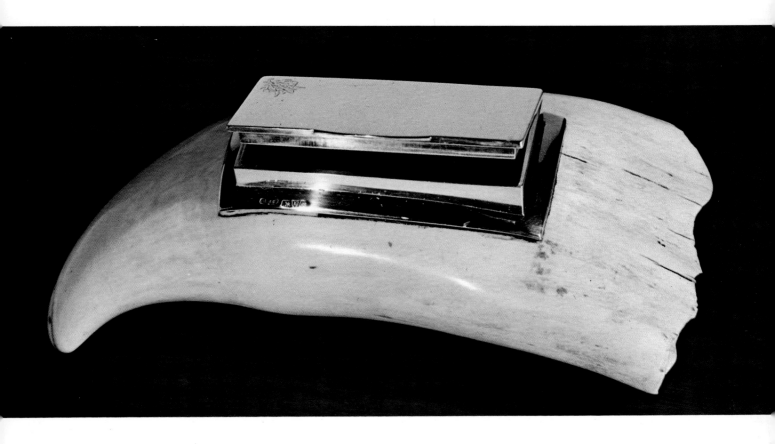

Photographs of President Kennedy at his desk show that this big whale's tooth with a handsomely monogrammed silver box set into the top occupied a place on the desk top for a time. English hallmarks and the imprint "Barretson-Piccadilly" would indicate a British origin of this fine piece.

The Sea from Whence We Came 7

There is a rapture on the lonely shore;
There is society, where none intrudes,
By the deep sea, and music in its roar:
I love not man the less, but Nature more.
— BYRON, *Childe Harold's Pilgrimage*

THE sea was never far from John F. Kennedy. In Boston and at the house on Cape Cod, the sea was forever at his elbow. Even the theater of his war was the sea. We know that in moments of stress and pressure during the days of his Presidency, the doodlings that Evelyn Lincoln, his secretary, found on his scratch pads often tended to be sailboats. Away from the sea, it was ever present in his heart and in his mind. His White House office was filled with reminders of the world of sailors and sailing ships. Each of them silently recalled moments of courage in American history.

This becomes especially evident in his choice of scrimshawed whales' teeth in the collection. The subject matter etched on the whale's tooth had to be patriotic to interest Kennedy — pictures such as the Bunker Hill Monument, Independence Hall, the President's House; scrimshawed portraits of historic figures — Washington, Lincoln, Grant, John Adams, Stephen Decatur and Alexander Hamilton; scrimshawed patriotic symbols— figures of liberty, justice with her scales, the American flag, the Seal of the President of the United States; and scrimshawed sailing ships — ships of the old Navy, frigates of the War of 1812, ships that sailed hundreds of thousands of miles over the years like the lucky U.S.S. *Vincennes,* whaleships like the gallant old *Hector,* and scenes of whaling combat.

We know that Kennedy was well aware of all the other sorts of scrimshaw the whalemen made: the handsome whalebone and ivory walking sticks, the ingenious pie crimpers or jagging wheels, the elaborate wool winders or swifts, sentimental busks and all the other hundreds of ornamental or useful items made on the whaleships. But articles of this sort, desirable as they may be to collectors of more catholic taste in scrimshaw, had no place in the Kennedy collection in the White House.

Kennedy was highly selective in his choice of the scrimshawed whales' teeth that sat before him on his desk and on the shelves and tabletops in the Oval Office. They were trophies taken in fierce combat with monstrous sperm whales. They were symbols of courage; they were symbols of triumph and tragedy. In them was a power to nurture courage and character in the receptive beholder.

Even when a President can get away from his desk from time to time, he cannot escape from the continuing duties of his job. Wherever he goes, the job goes with him, along with numerous staff aides, secretaries, Secret Service men and an army of reporters and photographers. Privacy for the President and his family is virtually out of the question. Camp David, the Presidential retreat in the Catoctin Mountains of Maryland, is run by the Navy as a military base, and so it offers the most privacy. But of all the places President Kennedy went for relaxation, his home at Hyannis Port, the house on Nantucket Sound, was his favorite.

There is fresh salt air to breathe as soon as you step off the plane. Slip on a sweater or an old jacket, go out to look at the sea and the beach in front of the house to make sure it's still there, and it's a whole new world.

The President's House in Washington is an elegant and gracious home with ample grounds, but it could never give Kennedy what he found at the Cape: sky, sea and beach. The great wash of ocean air, the openness, the feeling of grass or beach sand under foot. And all the familiar sounds of the seashore: waves that lap with a hollow thunking sound against boats, the motor of a fisherman going out, the night heron quawking along the shore, the sound of rain on the roof.

The view from the house at Hyannis Port, the far, watery horizon and the parallel beach in the middle ground, is in itself restful. It was the French painter, Seurat, who theorized that long horizontal lines convey a mood of repose and serene tranquility to the viewer.

Hyannis Port was not, however, an escape. The problems of his Office went right along on the plane from Washington to the Cape. Some of the physical pressure was off, to be sure: the endless round of appointments, conferences, phone calls and posing with visitors from Pocatello. Probably every President has complained at one time or another as Kennedy did of being "too busy to think." But sitting on the sunny terrace at the summer White House or going for a walk by himself along the beach perhaps gave Kennedy an uninterrupted solitude, a quiet time to contemplate and muse over the problems of his job.

Sailing, swimming, or walking the beach where he played as a child restored and refreshed John Kennedy, "recharged his batteries," in that mundane but apt expression. Kennedy's feeling for the sea was well expressed in his own words when he proposed a toast to the crew of *Gretel* and the crew of *Weatherly* at the Australian Ambassador's dinner for the America's Cup crews at Newport in September, 1962:

I really don't know why it is that all of us are so committed to the sea, except I think it's because in addition to the fact that the sea changes, and the

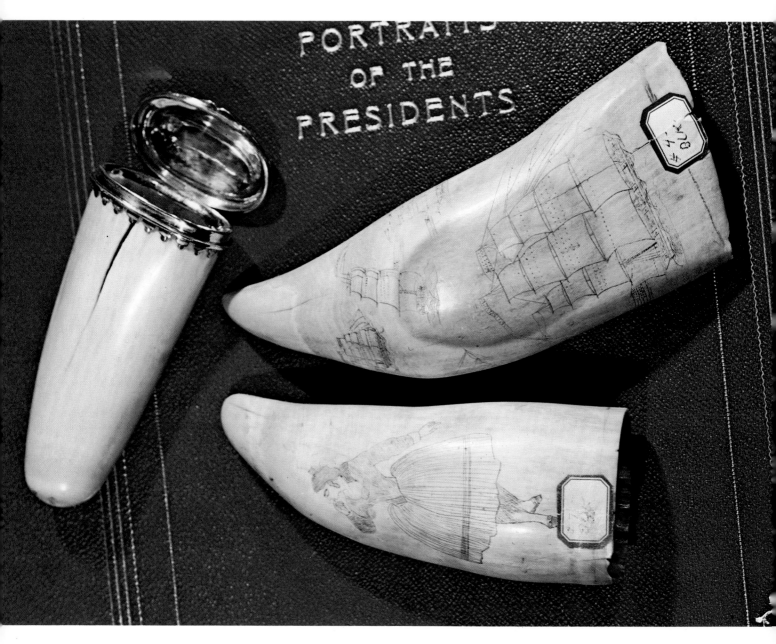

Two whales' teeth and a nice snuffbox carved from a whale's tooth arrived at the White House for Kennedy's consideration at the very time of the fatal trip to Texas. The President never saw these items. Evelyn Lincoln said that the consignor later inquired as to their disposition, offering of course to take back the pieces. Mrs. Lincoln stated that the family decided to retain them, however, to go with the rest of the scrimshaw collection to the Kennedy Library. It is the writer's feeling that Kennedy might have purchased the whale's tooth covered with sailing ships, but the other pieces would not seem to be the kind of scrimshaw that interested the President.

light changes, and the ships change, it's because we all came from the sea. And it is an interesting biological fact that all of us have in our veins the exact same percentage of salt in our blood that exists in the ocean, and, therefore, we have salt in our blood, in our sweat, in our tears. We are tied to the ocean. And when we go back to the sea — whether it be to sail or to watch it — we are going back from whence we came. [1]

The ocean is life. Life is an eternal conflict between good and evil. Courage and intelligence, self-reliance and character, qualities that lead to right action must be sought within ourselves if we would have them in our leaders. Emerson, in his essay "Self-Reliance," thought:

The force of character is cumulative. All the foregone days of virtue work their health into this. What makes the majesty of the heroes of the senate and the field, which so fills the imagination? The consciousness of a train of great days and victories behind. They shed an united light on the advancing actor. He is attended as by a visible escort of angels. That is it which throws thunder into Chatham's voice, and the dignity into Washington's port, and America into Adams's eye. Honor is venerable to us because it is no ephemeris. It is always ancient virtue. We worship it today because it is not of today. We love it and pay it homage, because it is not a trap for our love and homage, but is self-dependent, self-derived, and therefore of an immaculate pedigree, even if shown in a young person. [2]

Yet in the sunless depths of the ocean there is and always has been the "violent, ungovernable, unintelligent destroyer" [3] that Melville pondered, "the unintelligent brute force that lies at the bottom of society," [4] as Emerson expressed it.

"The magnetism which all original action exerts is explained when we inquire the reason of self-trust," Emerson wrote. "Who is

This whale's tooth we take to be a memorial piece honoring a whaleman killed by a sperm whale on July 4, 1841, the date at the top of
the tooth. Flowers surround the carefully stippled but undecipherable
name of the sailor. At the base of the tooth a topsail schooner ap-
proaches a shoreline extending around the tooth, where an American
lighthouse stands. "Forget me not" is the pleading inscription. On
the reverse side is etched the whaleman's enormous adversary, a spouting sperm whale, titled "There she blows." Perhaps more information
will turn up some day on what seems to have been a tragedy of Independence Day in 1841.

the Trustee? What is the aboriginal self, on which a universal reliance may be grounded? What is the nature and power of that science-baffling star, without parallax, without calculable elements, which shoots a ray of beauty even into trivial and impure actions, if the least mark of independence appear?" [5]

Emerson sought the reason for self-trust, that same independent courage in action whose source Kennedy explored, studied and found to be something of an enigma in the makeup of the men he portrayed in *Profiles in Courage*. Emerson's answer was this:

"The inquiry leads us to that source, at once the essence of genius, of virtue, and of life, which we call Spontaneity or Instinct. We denote this primary wisdom as Intuition, whilst all later teachings are tuitions. In that deep force, the last fact behind which analysis cannot go, all things finds their common origin." [6]

Spontaneity, or instinct, this primary wisdom called intuition, motivated the men of John F. Kennedy's book, and it was in the core of the author himself when he wrote:

"The courage of life is often a less dramatic spectacle than the courage of a final moment; but it is no less a magnificent mixture of triumph and tragedy. A man does what he must — in spite of personal consequences, in spite of obstacles and dangers and pressures — and that is the basis of all human morality." [7]

Now small fowls flew screaming over the yet yawning gulf; a sullen white surf beat against its steep sides; then all collapsed, and the great shroud of the sea rolled on as it rolled five thousand years ago.
— HERMAN MELVILLE, Moby Dick

Acknowledgments

THIS book began to take shape when President John F. Kennedy gave me permission to have photographs made of his scrimshaw collection as it was displayed in his office at the White House in early 1963. After his death, Mrs. Kennedy gave her gracious consent to photograph the pieces he later acquired. The entire collection was stored at that time in the National Archives Building in the care of Dr. Herman Kahn. A whale's tooth incised with a portrait of President Kennedy by Milton K. Delano was not available for photographing. The picture of this tooth is used through the courtesy of the *New Bedford Standard-Times*.

Most photographs of scrimshaw have been of the "catalogue" variety, and they rarely do justice to the subject matter. I would therefore pay particular tribute to Alan Fontaine, who photographed the Kennedy scrimshaw pieces for what they are — excitingly beautiful examples of the whaleman's art. Most of the photographs were made on a Saturday afternoon in the President's office. We were warned that we would have to be out of the office — cameras, cables, lighting equipment and all — within three minutes if President Kennedy should suddenly require the room. The many beautiful pictures in this book, taken under that kind of pressure, indicate the sure taste and craftsmanship of a great photographer. We would not really appreciate Kennedy's interest in scrimshaw without these lovely pictures by Fontaine. They constitute a treasury of visual pleasure.

Special thanks go to LeMoyne Billings, who helped the President so much in building his collection, and whose recollections have assisted greatly in recording John Kennedy's interest in scrimshaw. I am grateful to Nancy Tuckerman, Mrs. Kennedy's secretary, and to David Powers, the President's White House aide, for all their helpful cooperation. I thank Milton K. Delano and George Wintress, both experienced advisers to President Kennedy in the field of scrimshaw, for informative conversations.

Every writer on whaling scrimshaw owes an everlasting debt of acknowledgment to the late Clifford Ashley, whaleman, artist and writer, whose chapter on scrimshaw in his book, *The Yankee Whaler,* set a bench mark for all the writers on scrimshaw who followed him. Many published articles on scrimshaw have a familiar ring to those well-versed in the subject. A great deal has been written about whaling, but there is, in fact, no substantial body of literature on scrimshaw per se. The same sources are quoted again and again, but it will, perhaps, seem fresh to the newcomer to scrimshaw.

Much background information on a number of identifiable scrimshawed teeth in the Kennedy collection has come from the careful researching and writings of Edouard Stackpole, particularly his *Scrimshaw at Mystic Seaport* and his compendium of whaling lore, *The Sea-Hunters.* The writings of Henry Beetle Hough, the "country editor" of the renowned *Vineyard Gazette* and a notable whaling historian, have helped greatly to make the old-time whalemen come alive for this writer. I am grateful to Peter Stanford, president of New York's

124

South Street Seaport Museum, for his help in identifying various types of ships etched on the Kennedy scrimshaw and in matters of nautical nomenclature.

Portions of the material in this book appeared in *American Heritage,* October 1964, written with the collaboration of Croswell Bowen, whose friendly counsel has aided greatly in preparing this expanded picture of John F. Kennedy, scrimshaw collector. I also thank Vance Packard, a writer's writer and my Chappaquiddick Island neighbor, whose leading questions, advice and encouragement helped get this manuscript off the ground; Susan Barnes Walker, who devoted long hours to its research and typing; Stanley Hart, whose nautical interest brought this book to the attention and the invaluable editing hand of Larned Bradford at Little, Brown.

CLARE BARNES, JR.

Chappaquiddick Island
Edgartown, Massachusetts

Notes

2. THE WHALEMAN'S ART

1. Ashley, Clifford W., *The Yankee Whaler*. New York: Halcyon House, 1942.
2. Hart, Joseph C., *Miriam Coffin*. San Francisco: H. R. Coleman, 1872.
3. Stackpole, Edouard A., *Scrimshaw at Mystic Seaport*. Connecticut: Marine Historical Association, 1958.
4. Lieberson, Goddard, ed., *John Fitzgerald Kennedy . . . As We Remember Him*. New York: Macmillan Company, 1965.
5. Shepard, Tazewell, Jr., *John F. Kennedy, Man of the Sea*. New York: William Morrow & Company, 1965.
6. Shapiro, Irwin, and Stackpole, Edouard A., *The Story of Yankee Whaling*. New York: American Heritage Publishing Company, 1959.
7. Barbeau, Marius, "All Hands Aboard Scrimshawing," *The American Neptune*, vol. XII, no. 2., 1952.
8. Hall, Charles F., *Narrative of the Second Arctic Expedition, 1864–1869*. Washington, D.C.: U.S. Naval Observatory, Government Printing Office, 1879.
9. Crèvecoeur, J. Hector St. John de, *Letters from an American Farmer* (1782). New York: E. P. Dutton & Company, 1957.
10. Davis, William M., *Nimrod of the Sea, or the American Whaleman*. New York: Harper & Brothers, 1874.
11. Cheever, Henry T., *The Whale and His Captors*. New York: Harper & Brothers, 1850.
12. Brown, James Templeman, *Fishery Industries of the United States*, vol. II, section V. Washington, D.C.: Government Printing Office, 1887.

3. SCRIMSHAW AND SALT WATER

1. Crèvecoeur, J. Hector St. John de, *Letters from an American Farmer* (1782). New York: E. P. Dutton & Company, 1957.
2. Purchas, Samuel, *Purchas: His Pilgrimes*, vol. XIX. Glasgow: James MacLehose & Sons, 1905–07.
3. Sorensen, Theodore C., *Kennedy*. New York: Harper & Row, 1965.

4. HISTORY ETCHED ON IVORY

1. White, Theodore H., "For President Kennedy, an Epilogue," Life, November 1963.
2. Horgan, Tom, *Old Ironsides: The Story of the U.S.S. Constitution.* Boston: Burdette, 1963.
3. Shepard, Tazewell, Jr., *John F. Kennedy, Man of the Sea.* New York: William Morrow & Company, 1965.
4. Steele, Joel Dorman, *Barnes' Centenary History. One Hundred Years of Independence.* New York: A. S. Barnes & Company, 1876.
5. Morris, Richard B., ed., *Encyclopedia of American History.* New York: Harper & Row, 1965.

5. SCRIMSHAWED SYMBOLS OF COURAGE

1. Melville, Herman, *Moby Dick, or The White Whale.* New York: The New American Library, 1961.
2. Ashley, Clifford W., *The Yankee Whaler.* New York: Halcyon House, 1942.
3. Stackpole, Edouard A., *The Sea-Hunters.* Philadelphia: J. B. Lippincott Company, 1953.
4. Shepard, Tazewell, Jr., *John F. Kennedy, Man of the Sea.* New York: William Morrow & Company, 1965.
5. Bowen, Croswell, "The Scrimshaw Collector," *American Heritage,* vol. XV, no. 6., 1964.
6. Lieberson, Goddard, ed., *John Fitzgerald Kennedy . . . As We Remember Him.* New York: Macmillan Company, 1965.
7. Kennedy, John F., *Profiles in Courage.* New York: Harper & Brothers, 1956.
8. Ibid.

6. SCRIMSHAW AND CREATIVE EXPRESSION

1. Shepard, Tazewell, Jr., *John F. Kennedy, Man of the Sea.* New York: William Morrow & Company, 1965.
2. Lieberson, Goddard, ed., *John Fitzgerald Kennedy . . . As We Remember Him.* New York: Macmillan Company, 1965.
3. Lubbock, Basil, *The Arctic Whalers.* Glasgow: Brown Son & Ferguson, Ltd., 1955.

7. THE SEA FROM WHENCE WE CAME

1. Shepard, Tazewell, Jr., *John F. Kennedy, Man of the Sea.* New York: William Morrow & Company, 1965.
2. Emerson, Ralph Waldo, *Works of Ralph Waldo Emerson.* London: George Routledge & Sons, 1883.
3. Melville, Herman, *Moby Dick, or The White Whale.* New York: The New American Library, 1961.
4. Emerson, Ralph Waldo, *Works of Ralph Waldo Emerson.* London: George Routledge & Sons, 1883.
5. Ibid.
6. Ibid.
7. Kennedy, John F., *Profiles in Courage.* New York: Harper & Brothers, 1956.